I0008600

Practical Python Projects: Build Real-World Applications with Python

A Step-by-Step Guide to Hands-On Python Programming

BOOZMAN RICHARD

BOOKER BLUNT

All rights reserved

No part of this book may be reproduced, distributed, or transmitted in any form or by any means without the prior written permission of the publisher, except in the case of brief quotations embodied in critical reviews and certain other noncommercial uses permitted by right law.

Table of Content

TABLE OF CONTENTS

INTRODUCTION

Practical Python Projects: Build Real-World Applications with Python

Welcome to **"Practical Python Projects: Build Real-World Applications with Python"**, a comprehensive guide designed to take you from the fundamentals of Python programming to building complex, real-world applications. Whether you are a beginner looking to understand Python from the ground up, or an experienced developer eager to expand your skills, this book will guide you through a structured learning journey with hands-on projects that bring concepts to life.

Python has firmly established itself as one of the most versatile and powerful programming languages in the world. From web development and data analysis to machine learning and IoT, Python is used in virtually every field of software development. This book is focused on giving you practical experience with Python by building applications that you can use and modify. The goal is not just to teach you Python syntax, but to ensure you understand how to apply your knowledge to solve real-world problems.

Why This Book?

As a developer, it's easy to get lost in theory and endless tutorials that don't result in something tangible. This book takes a different approach. Each chapter is structured to introduce new concepts and then immediately apply them in projects that challenge you to think critically and creatively.

- **Hands-on Projects**: You won't just be writing "Hello, World" programs. You will work on creating practical applications that real users could use. Whether it's a weather monitoring system, an e-commerce platform, or an IoT device, the projects in this book mirror the kinds of applications you will encounter in the real world.
- **Step-by-Step Instructions**: Every project includes clear, actionable instructions, and detailed explanations of how the code works. This ensures that you not only know how to build the application but also understand why certain design patterns, libraries, and tools are used.
- **Broad Range of Topics**: The book covers a broad spectrum of Python's capabilities. You'll learn how to:

- o Set up Python environments and tools like Git for version control.
- o Build web applications with Flask and Django.
- o Interact with cloud platforms such as AWS, Google Cloud, and Heroku.
- o Use Docker for containerization and Kubernetes for scaling applications.
- o Work with IoT devices and real-time applications.

- **Focus on Clean, Maintainable Code**: Throughout the book, there is a strong emphasis on writing clean, modular, and maintainable code. You'll learn how to structure projects effectively, apply Object-Oriented Programming (OOP) principles, and ensure your applications are secure and scalable.

- **Real-World Use Cases**: By the end of this book, you'll have developed projects that are not only practical but also scalable. These projects can serve as the foundation for your portfolio, whether you're starting a new career or looking to advance in your current role.

Who Should Read This Book?

This book is aimed at both beginners and intermediate Python developers who want to take their skills to the next level. It's ideal for anyone who:

- Has a basic understanding of Python (variables, loops, functions) and wants to learn how to build full-scale applications.
- Wants to understand how to structure code, build databases, handle APIs, and deploy applications in the cloud.
- Is eager to learn industry-standard practices such as version control, debugging, and testing.
- Enjoys learning by doing and wants to work on projects that are both challenging and rewarding.

If you're ready to move beyond the basics and start building real-world applications, this book is for you. You'll not only build projects that demonstrate your Python skills, but you'll also gain practical knowledge that will be invaluable in the workplace or when working on freelance projects.

What You'll Learn

- **Foundations of Python**: You'll start by mastering Python basics such as data structures, functions, and object-oriented programming. As we move forward, you will encounter more advanced concepts like working with cloud platforms, web frameworks (Flask, Django), and databases.

- **Working with APIs and Real-Time Data**: Learn how to interact with third-party APIs to retrieve data and integrate it into your applications. You'll also work with WebSockets for real-time communication.

- **Building Web Applications**: Create robust web applications using Flask and Django. You will understand the full web development cycle, from building models and views to deploying the app.

- **Cloud Computing and Deployment**: Dive into cloud computing with Python, and learn how to deploy and scale applications using platforms like AWS, Heroku, Docker, and Kubernetes.

- **Advanced Topics**: Towards the end of the book, you will explore more specialized topics such as IoT

(Internet of Things), machine learning integration, and building scalable applications.

The Journey Ahead

This book is designed to be a learning experience where you start with the basics, but by the end, you'll have the skills and confidence to build complex Python applications. Here's a brief overview of the journey:

- **Chapter 1-5**: You'll learn the core Python concepts, including setting up your development environment, working with data, and building basic applications.
- **Chapter 6-10**: These chapters delve into web development and real-time applications, where you will build Flask-based web apps, learn about APIs, and explore cloud-based services.
- **Chapter 11-15**: You will explore data science tools, machine learning basics, and real-time communication using WebSockets.
- **Chapter 16-20**: These chapters focus on application deployment, security, and scalability, providing you with the tools to build and maintain production-ready Python applications.

- **Chapter 21-25**: The final chapters cover more advanced topics like cloud computing, Docker, Kubernetes, and deploying applications to cloud services, bringing everything together for real-world deployment.

By the end of this book, you will have built multiple applications, learned industry best practices, and gained confidence in deploying and maintaining production-level Python projects.

Why This Book Stands Out

- **Practical Approach**: This book focuses on hands-on learning and real-world applications. The projects are designed to give you practical experience that you can apply immediately.
- **Comprehensive Coverage**: From basic programming concepts to advanced deployment techniques, this book covers a wide range of topics necessary to be a successful Python developer.
- **Industry Standards**: The book emphasizes the use of industry-standard tools and practices such as version control with Git, testing, security, and cloud

computing, making it highly relevant for today's software development landscape.

Get Ready to Build: Whether you're interested in building web applications, working with APIs, automating tasks, or diving into IoT, this book provides the resources and guidance to make your Python projects come to life. Each chapter is designed to build your skills gradually, helping you create a portfolio of real-world Python applications that showcase your abilities.

Let's start building!

CHAPTER 1

INTRODUCTION TO PYTHON PROGRAMMING

Overview:

Python is a versatile, powerful, and beginner-friendly programming language that has gained tremendous popularity in the tech world due to its simplicity and wide range of applications. Whether you're looking to build web applications, automate tasks, analyze data, or develop machine learning models, Python is a go-to language for many industries and projects.

In this chapter, we will provide an introduction to Python, explain its key features, and showcase why it's ideal for building real-world applications. By the end of the chapter, you'll be familiar with the Python language, its syntax, and its basic building blocks, all of which are essential for embarking on your Python programming journey.

Topics Covered:

1. Python Basics: Variables, Data Types, and Operators

Python's simplicity and readability make it a great first language for beginners, but it's also powerful enough for experts to build complex applications. Here's a brief overview of Python's fundamental elements.

- **Variables**: Variables are used to store data that can be referenced and manipulated in a program. In Python, variables do not require an explicit declaration to reserve memory space. The declaration happens when you assign a value to a variable.
    - Example:

      python

      ```
      x = 5  # 'x' is a variable storing
      the integer value 5
      name = "Alice"  # 'name' is a
      variable storing the string "Alice"
      ```

- **Data Types**: Python supports a variety of data types, including numbers, strings, and more complex types such as lists and dictionaries.
    - Examples of data types:
        - **Integers**: 5, -23

16

- **Floating point numbers**: `3.14, -9.5`
- **Strings**: `"Hello, world!"`
- **Booleans**: `True, False`
- **Lists**: `[1, 2, 3]`
- **Dictionaries**: `{"key": "value"}`

- **Operators**: Operators are used to perform operations on variables and values. Python supports several types of operators:

  - **Arithmetic Operators** (e.g., +, -, *, /)

  ```python
  python

  a = 10
  b = 5
  print(a + b)    # Output: 15
  ```

  - **Comparison Operators** (e.g., ==, !=, >, <)
  - **Logical Operators** (e.g., and, or, not)

---

2. Python Syntax and Structure

The syntax of a programming language defines the set of rules that determine how programs are written. Python's syntax is clean and straightforward, making it easier to read and write code.

- **Indentation**: Python uses indentation (whitespace) to define code blocks, making it visually clear and concise.

17

- Example:

```python
if x > 5:
    print("x is greater than 5")   # This line is part of the if block
```

- **Comments**: Comments are used to explain code and are ignored by the Python interpreter. You can use single-line comments with the # symbol or multi-line comments with triple quotes (''' or """).
  - Example:

```python
# This is a comment
print("Hello, World!")   # This will print to the console
```

- **Code Blocks**: Code blocks (or control flow structures like loops, conditionals) are created using indentation rather than curly braces {} or other symbols.
  - Example of a conditional statement:

```python
if x > 5:
    print("Greater")
```

18

```
else:
    print("Smaller or equal")
```

---

3. First Python Program: "Hello, World!"

A good way to start learning any programming language is to write the classic "Hello, World!" program. This program simply prints the message "Hello, World!" to the screen, demonstrating how to interact with the output.

- **Code**:

```python
print("Hello, World!")
```

- **Explanation**:
  - `print()` is a built-in Python function that outputs text or other types of data to the screen.
  - When you run this code, the Python interpreter will display the message on the console.
- **Running the Program**: To run this program:
  1. Write the code in a file with a `.py` extension (e.g., `hello_world.py`).
  2. Open a terminal or command prompt.

3. Type `python hello_world.py` to run the program (make sure Python is installed and properly configured on your machine).

---

4. Overview of Python's Role in Real-World Applications

Python is one of the most versatile languages available today. Its applications span across various domains, from simple automation scripts to complex artificial intelligence models.

- **Web Development**: With frameworks like Django and Flask, Python is widely used in building dynamic web applications and APIs.
- **Data Science and Analytics**: Libraries like Pandas, NumPy, and Matplotlib make Python the go-to language for analyzing and visualizing data.
- **Machine Learning**: Libraries like TensorFlow, Keras, and scikit-learn allow Python to be used in machine learning and AI development.
- **Automation**: Python's simplicity and ease of use make it ideal for automating repetitive tasks, from file management to web scraping.
- **Game Development**: Python can also be used in game development with libraries like Pygame.
- **Scripting and System Automation**: Python is often used to write scripts for system administration and automation.

Python's wide range of applications makes it a valuable skill for developers, data scientists, engineers, and more. In this book, you will explore how to use Python to build real-world applications, learning how to apply Python to various problems and scenarios.

Conclusion:

In this chapter, we've covered the essential basics of Python, including how to set up the environment, work with variables and data types, understand syntax, and write your first Python program. As you progress through this book, you'll dive deeper into more complex topics, but these foundational skills are crucial for understanding how Python works and how to build real-world applications effectively. The following chapters will explore practical projects and real-life applications, building on the knowledge you've gained here.

CHAPTER 2

SETTING UP YOUR DEVELOPMENT ENVIRONMENT

Overview:

In this chapter, we will guide you through the process of setting up your development environment for Python programming. Properly configuring your system is crucial for a smooth development experience. We'll cover how to install Python, set up an Integrated Development Environment (IDE), get started with Python virtual environments, and introduce some basic debugging techniques that will help you when things go wrong. By the end of this chapter, you will have a fully functioning environment, ready to write and run Python code effectively.

Topics Covered:

1. Installing Python

Before you can start programming in Python, you need to install the Python interpreter on your computer. Here's how you can do that:

- **Step 1: Download Python**
    1. Go to the official Python website: https://www.python.org/downloads/.
    2. Choose the appropriate version for your operating system (Windows, macOS, or Linux).
    3. Download the latest version of Python (as of now, Python 3.x is the recommended version).
- **Step 2: Install Python**
    - **For Windows**:
        1. Run the downloaded installer.
        2. Make sure to check the box that says **"Add Python to PATH"** during installation. This ensures that Python is accessible from the command line.
        3. Click on **Install Now** and follow the on-screen instructions.
    - **For macOS**:
        1. Open the `.pkg` installer and follow the prompts to install Python.
        2. You may also consider using a package manager like Homebrew (`brew install python`) for a simpler installation process.
    - **For Linux**:
        1. On most Linux distributions, Python comes pre-installed. You can check if

23

Python is installed by running `python3 --version` in the terminal.

2. If Python is not installed, you can use a package manager to install it. For example:

   - On Ubuntu: `sudo apt-get install python3`

- **Step 3: Verify Installation** After installation, you can verify that Python is installed correctly by opening a terminal or command prompt and typing:

```bash
```

```
python --version   # For Windows and macOS
python3 --version  # For Linux
```

You should see the installed Python version displayed.

---

2. Setting Up an IDE (PyCharm, VS Code)

An Integrated Development Environment (IDE) is a tool that helps you write, edit, and debug your code efficiently. While there are many IDEs available, we'll focus on two of the most popular ones: PyCharm and Visual Studio Code (VS Code).

- **PyCharm**: PyCharm is a powerful, full-featured IDE specifically designed for Python development. It comes with built-in support for Python, excellent debugging tools, and code completion features.

- o **Installing PyCharm**:
    1. Go to the PyCharm website: https://www.jetbrains.com/pycharm/.
    2. Download the free Community version (or the Professional version if you prefer the paid features).
    3. Follow the installation instructions based on your operating system.
    4. Once installed, open PyCharm, and you are ready to start creating Python projects.

- o **Setting Up a Python Project in PyCharm**:
    1. Open PyCharm and select **Create New Project**.
    2. Choose the Python interpreter you just installed.
    3. Click **Create** and you can now start writing your Python code.

- **VS Code**: Visual Studio Code is a lightweight, flexible text editor that is great for Python development. It is highly customizable with extensions, including Python-specific tools.

    - o **Installing VS Code**:

1. Go to the VS Code website: https://code.visualstudio.com/.

2. Download and install the appropriate version for your operating system.

o **Setting Up Python in VS Code**:

1. After installing VS Code, open it and go to the Extensions view by clicking the Extensions icon on the sidebar.

2. Search for the **Python** extension by Microsoft and install it.

3. Open the terminal within VS Code (Terminal > New Terminal) and type `python --version` to ensure the Python interpreter is recognized.

4. To start a new Python project, simply create a new `.py` file and start coding.

• **IDE Comparison**:

o **PyCharm** is better for large-scale projects and provides advanced features like integrated testing, database management, and debugging.

o **VS Code** is lightweight, fast, and perfect for small to medium projects with the advantage of a wide range of extensions.

3. Introduction to Python Virtual Environments

A Python virtual environment is a self-contained directory that contains a Python installation for a particular version of Python, along with additional libraries. Virtual environments help to manage dependencies for different projects without conflicts.

- **Why Use Virtual Environments?**
  - Different projects might require different versions of libraries. Virtual environments allow you to create isolated environments for each project, avoiding issues where dependencies conflict.
- **Creating a Virtual Environment**:
  1. Open your terminal or command prompt.
  2. Navigate to the directory where you want to create the virtual environment.
  3. Run the following command to create a new virtual environment:

```bash

python -m venv myenv
```

This will create a folder named `myenv` in the current directory containing the virtual environment.

- **Activating the Virtual Environment**:
  - **On Windows**:

    ```bash
    myenv\Scripts\activate
    ```

  - **On macOS/Linux**:

    ```bash
    source myenv/bin/activate
    ```

- **Deactivating the Virtual Environment**: When you're done working in the virtual environment, you can deactivate it by running:

  ```bash
  deactivate
  ```

- **Installing Libraries**: With the virtual environment activated, you can install libraries using `pip` without affecting other projects.
  - Example:

    ```bash
    pip install requests
    ```

4. Basic Debugging Techniques

As you start building more complex Python applications, debugging becomes an essential skill. Debugging helps you identify and fix errors in your code. In this section, we'll cover some basic debugging techniques.

- **Print Statements**: The simplest form of debugging is using `print()` statements to output the values of variables and track the flow of your program.

```python
def add_numbers(a, b):
    print(f"Adding {a} and {b}")    # Debugging output
    return a + b
```

- **Using the Python Debugger (pdb)**: Python's built-in `pdb` module allows you to set breakpoints and step through your code interactively.
  - o To start the debugger, insert the following line in your code:

```python
import pdb; pdb.set_trace()
```

- o This will stop the program execution at that line, allowing you to examine variables, step through the code, and continue execution.

- **IDE Debugging**:
  - o Both PyCharm and VS Code have built-in debugging tools. In PyCharm, you can set breakpoints by clicking on the gutter next to the line numbers. When you run the program in debug mode, it will stop at the breakpoints, allowing you to inspect variables and control execution flow.
  - o In VS Code, you can add breakpoints by clicking next to the line numbers. To start debugging, click on the debug icon in the left sidebar and select **Run and Debug**.

Conclusion:

In this chapter, we've set up the Python development environment by installing Python, configuring an IDE (PyCharm or VS Code), and creating Python virtual environments to manage dependencies. We also covered basic debugging techniques that will help you catch and fix issues in your code efficiently. With this setup in place, you're ready to start writing, testing, and refining Python applications in a clean and organized environment. The next chapter will dive deeper into the fundamentals of Python programming and set you up for success in building real-world applications.

CHAPTER 3

DATA STRUCTURES AND ALGORITHMS IN PYTHON

Overview:

In this chapter, we will explore the essential data structures in Python, which are fundamental to writing efficient programs. Data structures help us store, organize, and manipulate data effectively. We'll cover lists, tuples, dictionaries, and sets, which are the most commonly used data structures in Python. Additionally, we'll introduce basic algorithms for sorting and searching, essential for any developer. Finally, we'll provide an overview of algorithm complexity and explain Big O notation, which will help you analyze the efficiency of your code.

Topics Covered:

1. Lists, Tuples, Dictionaries, and Sets

Python provides a rich set of built-in data structures that are easy to use and versatile. Let's go over each of them in detail:

- **Lists**: Lists are ordered, mutable collections of elements. You can store any type of data (numbers, strings, other lists, etc.) in a list. Lists are one of the most commonly used data structures in Python because they are flexible and support many operations.

  o **Creating a List**:

  ```python
  python

  my_list = [1, 2, 3, 4, 5]
  ```

  o **Accessing List Elements**: You can access elements in a list by their index:

  ```python
  python

  print(my_list[0])  # Output: 1
  ```

  o **Modifying Lists**: Lists are mutable, meaning you can change their content:

  ```python
  python

  my_list[2] = 10  # Changes the value at index 2 to 10
  print(my_list)  # Output: [1, 2, 10, 4, 5]
  ```

  o **List Operations**:

33

- Appending an element:
  `my_list.append(6)`
- Removing an element:
  `my_list.remove(4)`
- Slicing: `my_list[1:3]` (returns elements from index 1 to 2)

- **Tuples**: Tuples are similar to lists but are immutable (cannot be changed after creation). Tuples are used to store data that should not be modified, such as coordinates or fixed collections.

  o **Creating a Tuple**:

  ```python
  my_tuple = (1, 2, 3)
  ```

  o **Accessing Elements**: Similar to lists, you can access tuple elements by index:

  ```python
  print(my_tuple[1])   # Output: 2
  ```

- **Dictionaries**: Dictionaries are unordered collections of key-value pairs. Each key in a dictionary must be unique, and you can use any immutable data type (e.g., strings, numbers) as keys. Dictionaries are ideal for situations where you need fast lookups based on a unique identifier.

34

- **Creating a Dictionary**:

```python
my_dict = {'name': 'Alice', 'age':
25}
```

- **Accessing Values**: Use the key to access the value associated with it:

```python
print(my_dict['name'])    # Output:
Alice
```

- **Adding or Modifying Items**:

```python
my_dict['age'] = 26  # Modify the age
my_dict['city'] = 'New York'  # Add
a new key-value pair
```

- **Sets**: Sets are unordered collections of unique elements. They are useful for eliminating duplicates or performing set operations like union, intersection, and difference.
  - **Creating a Set**:

```python
```

```
my_set = {1, 2, 3, 4}
```

- o **Set Operations**:
    - Union: `my_set1 | my_set2`
    - Intersection: `my_set1 & my_set2`
    - Difference: `my_set1 - my_set2`
- o **Important Note**: Sets do not allow duplicate values. For example:

```python
python
```

```
my_set = {1, 2, 2, 3}  # Output: {1,
2, 3} (duplicate 2 removed)
```

---

2. Sorting and Searching Algorithms

Sorting and searching are fundamental operations in computer science. Python provides built-in methods for sorting and searching, but understanding how these algorithms work at a fundamental level is important for optimizing performance.

- **Sorting Algorithms**: Sorting is the process of arranging data in a particular order (ascending or descending). Common sorting algorithms include Bubble Sort, Insertion Sort, Merge Sort, and Quick Sort.

- o **Built-in Sorting**: Python provides the `sorted()` function and the `.sort()` method for sorting lists:

  python

  ```
  my_list = [4, 2, 3, 1]
  sorted_list = sorted(my_list)    #
  Output: [1, 2, 3, 4]
  my_list.sort()  # Sorts the list in
  place
  ```

- o **Bubble Sort**: Bubble Sort repeatedly compares adjacent elements and swaps them if they are in the wrong order. It continues this process until the list is sorted.

  python

  ```
  def bubble_sort(arr):
      n = len(arr)
      for i in range(n):
          for j in range(0, n-i-1):
              if arr[j] > arr[j+1]:
                  arr[j], arr[j+1] =
  arr[j+1], arr[j]
      return arr
  ```

Time Complexity: O(n²)

- o **Quick Sort**: Quick Sort is a divide-and-conquer algorithm that divides the list into smaller sublists, sorts them, and then combines them.

python

```python
def quick_sort(arr):
    if len(arr) <= 1:
        return arr
    pivot = arr[0]
    less = [x for x in arr[1:] if x <= pivot]
    greater = [x for x in arr[1:] if x > pivot]
    return quick_sort(less) + [pivot] + quick_sort(greater)
```

Time Complexity: O(n log n) on average

- **Searching Algorithms**: Searching is the process of finding an element in a collection. Common searching algorithms include Linear Search and Binary Search.
  - o **Linear Search**: Linear Search checks each element of the list sequentially until it finds the target element.

python

```python
def linear_search(arr, target):
```

```
for i, value in enumerate(arr):
    if value == target:
        return i
return -1
```

o **Binary Search**: Binary Search works on sorted lists by repeatedly dividing the list in half and checking if the target is in the left or right half. It's much faster than Linear Search on large sorted datasets.

python

```
def binary_search(arr, target):
    low, high = 0, len(arr) - 1
    while low <= high:
        mid = (low + high) // 2
        if arr[mid] == target:
            return mid
        elif arr[mid] < target:
            low = mid + 1
        else:
            high = mid - 1
    return -1
```

3. Introduction to Algorithm Complexity (Big O Notation)

Understanding the time and space complexity of algorithms is crucial for optimizing your code, especially when dealing with large datasets. **Big O notation** is used to describe the performance or complexity of an algorithm.

- **Big O Notation**: Big O notation expresses the upper bound of the runtime complexity of an algorithm in terms of the input size. It describes how the runtime grows as the size of the input increases.
  - **O(1)**: Constant time complexity – the operation takes the same amount of time regardless of input size.
    - Example: Accessing an element in a list by index.
  - **O(n)**: Linear time complexity – the runtime grows linearly with the input size.
    - Example: Linear Search.
  - **O(n²)**: Quadratic time complexity – the runtime grows quadratically with the input size. This is common with algorithms that involve nested loops.
    - Example: Bubble Sort.
  - **O(log n)**: Logarithmic time complexity – the runtime grows logarithmically with the input

size. This is common in algorithms that divide the problem space in half at each step.

- Example: Binary Search.

o **O(n log n)**: Linearithmic time complexity – this is a combination of linear and logarithmic time, often seen in more efficient sorting algorithms like Quick Sort and Merge Sort.

- Example: Merge Sort.

Why Big O Matters: Understanding Big O helps you choose the right algorithm for the task and gives you a way to estimate how your program will scale with larger inputs. For instance, if you're processing a large dataset, an algorithm with $O(n^2)$ complexity will take much longer than one with O(n log n) complexity.

Conclusion:

In this chapter, we've introduced essential data structures in Python, including lists, tuples, dictionaries, and sets. We've also explored basic sorting and searching algorithms, which are fundamental to many applications. Finally, we've learned about algorithm complexity and Big O notation, an important concept for analyzing the efficiency of algorithms. With this knowledge, you're equipped to write efficient, optimized Python code that scales well with larger datasets and real-world applications.

CHAPTER 4

WORKING WITH FUNCTIONS

Overview:

In this chapter, we will dive deep into Python functions, which are essential for building reusable, modular, and efficient code. Functions allow you to encapsulate code into blocks that can be executed whenever needed. You'll learn how to define functions, understand function arguments and return values, explore variable scope, and discover advanced function features like lambda functions, decorators, and higher-order functions. By the end of this chapter, you will be able to write well-structured Python programs using functions for a variety of tasks.

Topics Covered:

1. Defining Functions

A function in Python is a block of code that only runs when it is called. Functions are defined using the `def` keyword, followed by the function name, parentheses, and a colon. The body of the function contains the logic that gets executed when the function is called.

- **Defining a Simple Function**:

python

```python
def greet():
    print("Hello, World!")

greet()   # Calls the function and prints "Hello, World!"
```

- **Function with Parameters**: Functions can take parameters, allowing you to pass data to them when calling. These parameters are used inside the function to perform tasks.

python

```python
def greet(name):
    print(f"Hello, {name}!")

greet("Alice")   # Output: Hello, Alice!
```

- **Function with Multiple Parameters**: Functions can take multiple parameters, and Python handles them sequentially.

python

```python
def add(a, b):
```

43

```
    return a + b

result = add(5, 3)
print(result)   # Output: 8
```

---

2. Arguments, Return Values, and Scope

- **Arguments**: Arguments are the values you pass to a function when you call it. In the previous examples, name, a, and b are arguments. Python provides several types of arguments:
    - ○ **Positional arguments**: The values are assigned to parameters based on their position.
    - ○ **Keyword arguments**: You can specify the parameter names explicitly when calling the function.

    python

    ```
    def greet(name, age):
        print(f"Hello, {name}! You are
    {age} years old.")

    greet(age=30,   name="Alice")       #
    Output: Hello, Alice! You are 30
    years old.
    ```

o **Default arguments**: You can specify default values for parameters. If no value is passed for that parameter, the default value is used.

python

```python
def greet(name, age=25):
    print(f"Hello, {name}! You are
{age} years old.")

greet("Alice")    # Output: Hello,
Alice! You are 25 years old.
```

- **Return Values**: Functions can return a value to the caller using the `return` keyword. Once the `return` statement is executed, the function terminates and passes the value back.

python

```python
def add(a, b):
    return a + b

result = add(5, 3)
print(result)  # Output: 8
```

- **Scope**: The scope of a variable refers to where it can be accessed in the program. There are two primary types of scope:

o **Local scope**: Variables defined inside a function are in the local scope and can only be accessed within that function.

python

```python
def example():
    x = 10   # 'x' is local to the
function
    print(x)  # Works fine
example()
print(x)   # Error: x is not defined
outside the function
```

o **Global scope**: Variables defined outside of any function are in the global scope and can be accessed throughout the program.

python

```python
x = 10   # Global variable

def example():
    print(x)    # Accessing global
variable

example()   # Output: 10
```

3. Lambda Functions

Lambda functions are small anonymous functions defined using the `lambda` keyword. Unlike regular functions defined with `def`, lambda functions are written in a single line and are typically used for short-term operations where defining a full function might seem overkill.

- **Syntax**:

```python
lambda arguments: expression
```

- **Example of a Lambda Function**: A lambda function that adds two numbers:

```python
add = lambda a, b: a + b
print(add(5, 3))   # Output: 8
```

- **Lambda Functions in Functions**: Lambda functions are commonly used as arguments for functions like `map()`, `filter()`, and `sorted()`:

```python
numbers = [1, 2, 3, 4, 5]
```

```
# Using lambda with map() to square each
number
squared_numbers = list(map(lambda x: x**2,
numbers))
print(squared_numbers)  # Output: [1, 4, 9,
16, 25]
```

---

4. Decorators and Higher-Order Functions

Decorators and higher-order functions are more advanced topics that allow you to modify or extend the functionality of functions in Python.

- **Higher-Order Functions**: A higher-order function is a function that takes another function as an argument or returns a function as a result.
  - o **Example**:

    python

    ```
    def greet(name):
        return f"Hello, {name}!"

    def apply_func(func, name):
        return func(name)

    result = apply_func(greet, "Alice")
    ```

48

```
print(result)      # Output:   Hello,
Alice!
```

- **Decorators**: A decorator is a higher-order function that allows you to modify or enhance another function without changing its code. Decorators are often used for logging, access control, memoization, and more.

  o **Basic Decorator Syntax**: A decorator is applied to a function using the @ symbol followed by the decorator name.

  python

```python
def decorator(func):
    def wrapper():
        print("Before        function
execution")
        func()
        print("After         function
execution")
    return wrapper

@decorator
def say_hello():
    print("Hello!")

say_hello()
# Output:
# Before function execution
```

49

```
# Hello!
# After function execution
```

- **Example: Timing a Function**: Here's a decorator that measures the execution time of a function:

python

```python
import time

def time_it(func):
    def wrapper(*args, **kwargs):
        start_time = time.time()
        result = func(*args, **kwargs)
        end_time = time.time()
        print(f"Execution time: {end_time - start_time} seconds")
        return result
    return wrapper

@time_it
def slow_function():
    time.sleep(2)

slow_function()  # Output: Execution time: 2.0xxxxxx seconds
```

o **Using Decorators with Arguments**: Decorators can also take arguments. In this case, you'll need an extra level of nesting.

```python
def repeat(n):
    def decorator(func):
        def             wrapper(*args,
**kwargs):
            for _ in range(n):
                func(*args,
**kwargs)
        return wrapper
    return decorator

@repeat(3)
def greet(name):
    print(f"Hello, {name}!")

greet("Alice")
# Output:
# Hello, Alice!
# Hello, Alice!
# Hello, Alice!
```

Conclusion:

In this chapter, we've explored Python functions in depth. Functions are the backbone of Python programming, allowing you to write modular, reusable, and efficient code. You learned how to define functions, handle function arguments and return values, and understand variable scope. We also covered lambda functions for short-term operations and examined advanced topics like decorators and higher-order functions, which are powerful tools for enhancing your Python programs. With these skills, you'll be well-equipped to write more sophisticated and organized Python code.

CHAPTER 5

OBJECT-ORIENTED PROGRAMMING (OOP) IN PYTHON

Overview:

Object-Oriented Programming (OOP) is a programming paradigm that is centered around the concept of "objects," which are instances of "classes." OOP helps organize and structure your code in a way that models real-world entities, making it easier to maintain, scale, and reuse code. This chapter will introduce you to the key concepts of OOP, including classes and objects, methods, attributes, inheritance, polymorphism, and encapsulation. By the end of this chapter, you'll be able to design and implement simple OOP-based applications in Python.

Topics Covered:

1. Classes and Objects

- **Classes**: A class is a blueprint for creating objects. It defines a set of attributes and behaviors that the objects created from it will have. In Python, you define a class using the `class` keyword.

- o **Defining a Class**:

  python

  ```python
  class Dog:
      # Attributes
      def __init__(self, name, breed):
          self.name = name
          self.breed = breed

      # Method (behavior)
      def bark(self):
          print(f"{self.name}        is
  barking!")
  ```

- o **Creating an Object**: An object is an instance of a class. After defining the class, you can create objects by calling the class as if it were a function.

  python

  ```python
  my_dog    =    Dog("Rex",    "German
  Shepherd")
  ```

- o **Accessing Attributes**: You can access object attributes using dot notation.

python

```
print(my_dog.name)   # Output: Rex
print(my_dog.breed)      #   Output:
German Shepherd
```

- o **Calling Methods**: You can call methods on objects using dot notation.

python

```
my_dog.bark()    # Output: Rex is
barking!
```

---

2. Methods, Attributes, and Inheritance

- **Attributes**: Attributes are variables that belong to a class. They are used to store data or properties of the object.
  - o **Instance Attributes**: These are specific to each instance of the class. They are usually defined in the __init__ method (the constructor).

python

```
class Car:
    def __init__(self, make, model):
        self.make = make
        self.model = model
```

55

- o **Class Attributes**: These belong to the class itself and are shared across all instances of the class.

python

```
class Car:
    wheels = 4    # Class attribute
(all cars have 4 wheels)
```

- **Methods**: Methods are functions defined within a class that describe the behaviors of an object. The first parameter of every method in a class is always `self`, which refers to the instance of the class.

  - o **Instance Methods**: These methods operate on the instance attributes.

python

```
class Car:
    def __init__(self, make, model):
        self.make = make
        self.model = model

    def start_engine(self):
        print(f"{self.make}
{self.model}'s    engine    is    now
running.")
```

  - o **Calling Methods**:

56

```
python
```

```
my_car = Car("Toyota", "Corolla")
my_car.start_engine()    # Output:
Toyota Corolla's engine is now
running.
```

- **Inheritance**: Inheritance allows you to define a new class that is a modified version of an existing class. The new class inherits the attributes and methods of the existing class, which makes it easier to reuse code.

  o **Basic Inheritance**:

```
python
```

```
class Animal:
    def __init__(self, name):
        self.name = name

    def speak(self):
        print(f"{self.name} makes a
sound.")

class Dog(Animal):
    def speak(self):
        print(f"{self.name} barks.")

my_dog = Dog("Rex")
my_dog.speak()  # Output: Rex barks.
```

o **Constructor Overriding**: A subclass can override the constructor of the parent class.

python

```python
class Dog(Animal):
    def __init__(self, name, breed):
        super().__init__(name)        #
Calling the parent class constructor
        self.breed = breed
```

3. Polymorphism and Encapsulation

- **Polymorphism**: Polymorphism allows objects of different classes to be treated as instances of the same class. It allows methods to have the same name but behave differently based on the object calling them.
  - o **Example**:

python

```python
class Animal:
    def speak(self):
        print("Animal     makes     a
sound.")

class Dog(Animal):
    def speak(self):
```

```
        print("Dog barks.")

class Cat(Animal):
    def speak(self):
        print("Cat meows.")

animals = [Dog(), Cat()]
for animal in animals:
    animal.speak()    # Output:  Dog
barks. Cat meows.
```

- **Encapsulation**: Encapsulation is the concept of restricting access to certain details of an object and only exposing the necessary functionalities. This is done using access modifiers. In Python, you can define "private" attributes and methods by prefixing them with an underscore (_) or double underscore (__).

  o **Private Attributes**:

  ```
  python
  ```

  ```
  class Person:
      def __init__(self, name, age):
          self.__name = name # Private
  attribute
          self.age = age

      def get_name(self):
  ```

```
        return self.__name  # Public
method    to    access    the    private
attribute
```

o **Accessing Private Attributes**:

python

```
person = Person("Alice", 30)
print(person.get_name())   # Output:
Alice
print(person.__name)       #   Error:
AttributeError (since it's private)
```

o **Getter and Setter Methods**: You can create getter and setter methods to control access to private attributes.

python

```
class Person:
    def __init__(self, name, age):
        self.__name = name
        self.__age = age

    def get_name(self):
        return self.__name

    def set_name(self, name):
        self.__name = name
```

60

4. Designing a Simple OOP Project

Let's bring everything together by designing a simple object-oriented project: a **Library Management System**. In this project, we'll use classes and objects to model a library system that allows adding books, checking out books, and displaying available books.

- **Step 1: Define the Book Class**

python

```python
class Book:
    def __init__(self, title, author,
available=True):
        self.title = title
        self.author = author
        self.available = available

    def check_out(self):
        if self.available:
            self.available = False
            print(f"Book    '{self.title}'
checked out.")
        else:
            print(f"Book '{self.title}' is
already checked out.")
```

61

```python
    def return_book(self):
        self.available = True
        print(f"Book          '{self.title}'
returned.")
```

- **Step 2: Define the Library Class**

python

```python
class Library:
    def __init__(self):
        self.books = []

    def add_book(self, book):
        self.books.append(book)

    def list_books(self):
        print("Available books:")
        for book in self.books:
            if book.available:
                print(f"- {book.title}  by
{book.author}")
```

- **Step 3: Using the Classes to Create Objects**

python

```python
# Creating a library
library = Library()
```

```python
# Creating books
book1 = Book("Python Programming", "John
Doe")
book2 = Book("Learn JavaScript", "Jane
Smith")

# Adding books to the library
library.add_book(book1)
library.add_book(book2)

# Listing available books
library.list_books()

# Checking out a book
book1.check_out()

# Returning a book
book1.return_book()

# Listing available books after checkout
library.list_books()
```

Conclusion:

In this chapter, we have introduced Object-Oriented Programming (OOP) in Python, which is essential for structuring your code in a more organized and scalable way. We covered key OOP concepts such as classes, objects, methods, attributes, inheritance, polymorphism, and encapsulation. By using OOP principles, you can build real-world applications that are easier to manage and extend. We also created a simple project, a library management system, to demonstrate how to apply these OOP concepts in a practical scenario. With these skills, you are now ready to tackle more complex OOP-based projects in Python.

CHAPTER 6

WORKING WITH FILES AND DIRECTORIES

Overview:

In this chapter, we will explore file input and output (I/O) operations in Python. Files are a fundamental part of many real-world applications, and Python provides easy-to-use tools for working with them. You will learn how to read from and write to files, handle exceptions when dealing with files, and work with directories and file paths. By the end of this chapter, you will apply your knowledge to build a file-based note-taking app, which will be a practical project to reinforce the concepts.

Topics Covered:

1. Reading and Writing Files

Python provides built-in functions to read from and write to files. These functions allow you to perform I/O operations with both text and binary files.

- **Opening a File**: Before reading from or writing to a file, you need to open it using Python's `open()` function. The `open()` function takes two arguments: the file name and the mode. The mode specifies the action to be performed (reading, writing, etc.).

  - **Reading a File**: The most common mode for reading files is `'r'` (read). If the file doesn't exist, Python will throw a `FileNotFoundError`.

    python

    ```python
    file = open('example.txt', 'r')   # Open file in read mode
    content = file.read()   # Reads the entire content of the file
    print(content)
    file.close()  # Always close the file after use
    ```

  - **Writing to a File**: To write to a file, you can use the `'w'` (write) or `'a'` (append) modes.

    - `'w'` will overwrite the file if it already exists, and create a new one if it doesn't.
    - `'a'` will add content to the end of the file without overwriting existing content.

    python

```
file = open('example.txt', 'w')    #
Open file in write mode
file.write("Hello, World!")  # Write
data to the file
file.close()
```

o **Reading Line by Line**: You can read a file line by line, which is especially useful for large files:

python

```
file = open('example.txt', 'r')
for line in file:
    print(line, end='')    # Prints
each line in the file
file.close()
```

o **Context Manager (with Statement)**: Instead of manually opening and closing files, you can use the with statement, which automatically closes the file when the block is exited.

python

```
with open('example.txt', 'r') as
file:
    content = file.read()
    print(content)
```

2. Handling File Exceptions

When working with files, errors are common, such as the file not existing, permission errors, or issues with file format. Python provides exception handling to gracefully handle these errors.

- **Using `try` and `except`**: If an error occurs when opening a file, Python will raise an exception. You can catch these exceptions using `try` and `except` blocks.

  o **Example**: Handling a `FileNotFoundError`:

  python

  ```python
  try:
      file                          =
  open('non_existent_file.txt', 'r')
      content = file.read()
  except FileNotFoundError:
      print("The file was not found.")
  finally:
      file.close()  # Always ensure the
  file is closed
  ```

- **Handling Other Exceptions**: You can catch multiple exceptions by specifying them in the `except` block.

  python

  ```python
  try:
  ```

```
    file = open('example.txt', 'r')
    content = file.read()
except FileNotFoundError:
    print("File not found!")
except IOError:
    print("An I/O error occurred.")
finally:
    file.close()
```

- **Context Manager and Exceptions**: When using the with statement to manage files, Python automatically handles closing the file, even in the event of an error.

python

```
try:
    with open('example.txt', 'r') as file:
        content = file.read()
except FileNotFoundError:
    print("The file was not found.")
```

---

3. Working with Directories and File Paths

In addition to file handling, Python also allows you to work with directories and file paths, which are important for organizing your files and navigating your file system.

- **Getting the Current Working Directory**: Python provides the os module, which includes useful functions for interacting with the file system.

```python
```

```python
import os
print(os.getcwd())    # Prints the current
working directory
```

- **Changing the Current Working Directory**: You can change the current directory using os.chdir().

```python
```

```python
os.chdir('/path/to/directory')    # Change
working directory
```

- **Listing Files in a Directory**: Use os.listdir() to list the files in a directory.

```python
```

```python
files = os.listdir('/path/to/directory')
print(files)
```

- **Joining Paths**: Use os.path.join() to safely join file paths, making your code cross-platform.

```python
```

```
path = os.path.join('folder', 'file.txt')
print(path)   # Output: folder/file.txt
```

- **Checking if a File or Directory Exists**: Use `os.path.exists()` to check if a file or directory exists.

python

```
if os.path.exists('example.txt'):
    print("File exists!")
else:
    print("File does not exist!")
```

- **Creating Directories**: Use `os.mkdir()` to create a new directory.

python

```
os.mkdir('new_folder')       #   Creates   a
directory named 'new_folder'
```

- **Removing Files and Directories**: Use `os.remove()` to delete a file and `os.rmdir()` to remove an empty directory.

python

```
os.remove('example.txt')    # Removes  the
file
```

71

```
os.rmdir('new_folder')  # Removes the empty
directory
```

---

4. Project: Creating a File-Based Note-Taking App

Now that we've covered reading and writing files, handling exceptions, and working with directories, let's put these concepts into practice by building a simple note-taking app.

- **Step 1: Define the Structure** The app will allow users to:
    o Add a note (write it to a file).
    o View all notes (read from the file).
    o Delete a note (remove it from the file).
- **Step 2: Create the NoteApp Class** We will define a NoteApp class that will handle all the functionality of the app.

```python

import os

class NoteApp:
    def                     __init__(self,
filename="notes.txt"):
        self.filename = filename

    def add_note(self, note):
        try:
```

```python
            with open(self.filename, 'a')
as file:
                file.write(note + "\n")
        print("Note             added
successfully!")
        except Exception as e:
            print(f"Error    adding    note:
{e}")

    def view_notes(self):
        try:
            with open(self.filename, 'r')
as file:
                notes = file.readlines()
                if notes:
                    print("Notes:")
                    for note in notes:

print(note.strip())
                else:
                    print("No          notes
found.")
        except FileNotFoundError:
            print("No notes file found.")
        except Exception as e:
            print(f"Error    reading    notes:
{e}")

    def delete_note(self, note):
```

```
        try:
            with open(self.filename, 'r')
as file:
                notes = file.readlines()
            with open(self.filename, 'w')
as file:
                for current_note in notes:
                    if
current_note.strip() != note:

file.write(current_note)
            print(f"Note '{note}' deleted
successfully!")
        except Exception as e:
            print(f"Error deleting note:
{e}")
```

- **Step 3: Create a Simple User Interface** Let's allow the user to interact with the app via the command line.

```python
def main():
    app = NoteApp()

    while True:
        print("\n--- Note-Taking App ---")
        print("1. Add a note")
        print("2. View notes")
        print("3. Delete a note")
```

```
print("4. Exit")

choice = input("Enter your choice
(1-4): ")

if choice == "1":
    note = input("Enter your note:
")
    app.add_note(note)
elif choice == "2":
    app.view_notes()
elif choice == "3":
    note = input("Enter the note to
delete: ")
    app.delete_note(note)
elif choice == "4":
    print("Goodbye!")
    break
else:
    print("Invalid choice, please
try again.")

if __name__ == "__main__":
    main()
```

- **Step 4: Running the Application** When you run the app, it will allow the user to:
  - o Add a note to notes.txt.
  - o View all notes stored in the file.

o   Delete a note by its content.

Conclusion:

In this chapter, we've covered the fundamental operations for working with files and directories in Python. You learned how to read from and write to files, handle exceptions during file operations, and navigate directories using the `os` module. Additionally, we applied these concepts by building a simple file-based note-taking app, which reinforces the practical usage of file I/O operations. With these skills, you can start building more advanced applications that manage data stored in files and directories.

CHAPTER 7

INTRODUCTION TO WEB SCRAPING WITH PYTHON

Overview:

Web scraping is a technique used to extract data from websites. It is an essential skill for gathering information from the web, whether for data analysis, research, or automation tasks. Python, with its powerful libraries such as BeautifulSoup and Selenium, makes web scraping accessible and efficient. In this chapter, you'll learn how to use these libraries to scrape static and dynamic websites, handle and store the scraped data in useful formats like CSV and JSON, and finally, build a real-world weather data scraper.

Topics Covered:

1. Using BeautifulSoup for Parsing HTML

BeautifulSoup is one of the most popular Python libraries for web scraping. It allows you to parse HTML and XML documents, navigate the document tree, and extract relevant data. Here's how you can use BeautifulSoup to scrape a static webpage:

- **Installing BeautifulSoup**: BeautifulSoup is part of the bs4 package, which you can install using pip:

bash

```
pip install beautifulsoup4
pip install requests  # To fetch the web
pages
```

- **Fetching Web Pages**: To scrape a website, you first need to fetch the webpage. The requests library is commonly used for this.

python

```
import requests
from bs4 import BeautifulSoup

url = "https://example.com"
response = requests.get(url)
soup    =    BeautifulSoup(response.text,
'html.parser')
```

- **Navigating the HTML Structure**: Once you have the HTML content in a BeautifulSoup object, you can use various methods to navigate the document and extract information.
    - **Find a Single Element**: Use soup.find() to locate the first occurrence of a tag.

78

python

```
title = soup.find('h1')   # Finds the
first <h1> tag
print(title.text)   # Prints the text
inside the <h1> tag
```

o **Find All Elements**: Use `soup.find_all()` to find all occurrences of a particular tag.

python

```
links = soup.find_all('a')   # Finds
all <a> tags
for link in links:
    print(link.get('href'))          #
Prints the href attribute of each <a>
tag
```

o **Using CSS Selectors**: You can also use CSS selectors to find elements.

python

```
content = soup.select('.content')   #
Selects    elements    with    class
"content"
for item in content:
    print(item.text)
```

- **Example of Web Scraping with BeautifulSoup**: Here's a simple example that scrapes the titles of articles from a blog:

```python
url = "https://example-blog.com"
response = requests.get(url)
soup    =    BeautifulSoup(response.text,
'html.parser')

articles    =    soup.find_all('h2',
class_='article-title')
for article in articles:
    print(article.text)
```

2. Scraping Dynamic Websites with Selenium

While BeautifulSoup works great for static websites, some websites load content dynamically using JavaScript. For such websites, Selenium is a powerful tool that can interact with JavaScript and render dynamic content.

- **Installing Selenium**: First, you need to install the `selenium` package and a web driver (such as ChromeDriver or GeckoDriver).

```bash
```

```
pip install selenium
```

Download ChromeDriver: If you're using Chrome, download the appropriate version of ChromeDriver from here.

- **Setting Up Selenium**: After installing Selenium, you need to set up a driver, which will control the browser. Here's how you can set it up for Chrome:

```python
python

from selenium import webdriver

# Set up the Chrome driver (make sure
ChromeDriver is in your PATH)
driver                                  =
webdriver.Chrome(executable_path='/path/t
o/chromedriver')

# Navigate to a webpage
driver.get("https://example.com")

# Wait for content to load (if necessary)
driver.implicitly_wait(10)  # Wait up to 10
seconds for elements to load
```

```
# Extract the page source after JavaScript
has executed
page_source = driver.page_source
```

- **Extracting Data with Selenium**: Once the page has loaded, you can extract data similarly to BeautifulSoup, but using Selenium's methods.

python

```python
from selenium import webdriver
from selenium.webdriver.common.by import By

driver = webdriver.Chrome(executable_path='/path/t
o/chromedriver')
driver.get("https://example.com")

# Example: Get the text of an element with
the ID "header"
header = driver.find_element(By.ID,
"header")
print(header.text)

# Example: Get all links on the page
links = driver.find_elements(By.TAG_NAME,
"a")
for link in links:
```

```
print(link.get_attribute('href'))

driver.quit()   # Close the browser window
```

3. Storing Scraped Data in CSV and JSON Formats

Once you've scraped data from a website, it's often useful to store it in a format that can be easily used for analysis or further processing. Two popular formats for storing data are CSV and JSON.

- **Storing Data in CSV Format**: The csv module in Python allows you to read from and write to CSV files easily. Here's how to write scraped data to a CSV file:

```python
python

import csv

# Define the data to be written
data = [
    ["Name", "Age", "City"],
    ["Alice", 25, "New York"],
    ["Bob", 30, "Los Angeles"]
]

# Writing to CSV file
```

```
with        open('data.csv',        mode='w',
newline='') as file:
    writer = csv.writer(file)
    writer.writerows(data)
```

- o **Reading Data from CSV**:

  python

  ```
  with open('data.csv', mode='r')  as
  file:
      reader = csv.reader(file)
      for row in reader:
          print(row)
  ```

- **Storing Data in JSON Format**: JSON is a popular format for data exchange. The `json` module in Python provides methods for reading and writing JSON data.

  - o **Writing Data to JSON**:

    python

    ```
    import json

    data = {"name": "Alice", "age": 25,
    "city": "New York"}

    # Writing to a JSON file
    with   open('data.json',   'w')   as
    json_file:
    ```

```
json.dump(data, json_file)
```

o **Reading Data from JSON:**

```
python
```

```
with open('data.json', 'r') as
json_file:
    data = json.load(json_file)
    print(data)
```

---

4. Project: Build a Weather Data Scraper

In this project, we will combine the techniques learned in this chapter to build a weather data scraper. This scraper will fetch weather information from a website and store it in a CSV or JSON file.

- **Step 1: Set Up the Scraper**: We'll scrape weather data from a weather website (e.g., `https://example-weather-site.com`), extract the city, temperature, and conditions, and store it in a CSV file.

  o **Using BeautifulSoup:**

  ```
  python
  ```

  ```
  import requests
  from bs4 import BeautifulSoup
  ```

```python
import csv

# Function to scrape weather data
def get_weather_data():
    url = 'https://example-weather-site.com'
    response = requests.get(url)
    soup = BeautifulSoup(response.text, 'html.parser')

    # Extract data
    city = soup.find('div', class_='city').text
    temperature = soup.find('span', class_='temp').text
    conditions = soup.find('span', class_='conditions').text

    return [city, temperature, conditions]

# Step 2: Write to CSV
weather_data = get_weather_data()
with open('weather_data.csv', mode='w', newline='') as file:
    writer = csv.writer(file)
```

```
    writer.writerow(["City",
"Temperature", "Conditions"])    #
Header row
    writer.writerow(weather_data)


print("Weather    data    saved    to
weather_data.csv")
```

- o **Using Selenium for Dynamic Content**: If the weather website is dynamically rendered, you can use Selenium to interact with the page and scrape the data:

python

```
from selenium import webdriver
from    selenium.webdriver.common.by
import By
import csv

driver                           =
webdriver.Chrome(executable_path='/
path/to/chromedriver')
driver.get('https://example-
weather-site.com')

# Wait for dynamic content to load
driver.implicitly_wait(10)
```

```python
city                        =
driver.find_element(By.CLASS_NAME,
'city').text
temperature                 =
driver.find_element(By.CLASS_NAME,
'temp').text
conditions                  =
driver.find_element(By.CLASS_NAME,
'conditions').text

# Save to CSV
with         open('weather_data.csv',
mode='w', newline='') as file:
    writer = csv.writer(file)
    writer.writerow(["City",
"Temperature",  "Conditions"])    #
Header row
    writer.writerow([city,
temperature, conditions])

print("Weather    data    saved    to
weather_data.csv")
driver.quit()
```

Conclusion:

In this chapter, we introduced web scraping using Python. You learned how to scrape static websites with BeautifulSoup and dynamic websites with Selenium. We also covered how to store scraped data in useful formats like CSV and JSON. Finally, we completed a project where you built a weather data scraper, putting all the concepts into practice. With this knowledge, you can now scrape data from various websites and store it for further analysis or use in your applications.

CHAPTER 8

INTRODUCTION TO WEB DEVELOPMENT WITH FLASK

Overview:

Flask is a lightweight and easy-to-use web framework for Python that allows developers to build web applications quickly and efficiently. In this chapter, we'll introduce you to Flask by setting up a basic Flask application and working with essential components such as routes, templates, forms, and databases. Flask's simplicity makes it ideal for beginners and experts alike, providing a solid foundation for building dynamic web applications. We'll also walk through a project where you'll build a simple personal blog, helping you solidify your understanding of web development with Flask.

Topics Covered:

1. Setting Up a Basic Flask Application

Flask allows you to create web applications with minimal setup. To begin working with Flask, you need to install it and set up a basic application.

- **Installing Flask**: You can install Flask using pip:

bash

```
pip install flask
```

- **Creating Your First Flask Application**: Flask applications are defined by creating an instance of the `Flask` class. Here's how you can set up a basic Flask app:

python

```
from flask import Flask

# Create a Flask application instance
app = Flask(__name__)

# Define a route and its associated
function
@app.route('/')
def home():
    return "Hello, World!"

# Run the app on the local development
server
if __name__ == "__main__":
    app.run(debug=True)
```

  o **Explanation**:

- Flask(__name__): Creates an instance of the Flask class. __name__ refers to the current module.
- @app.route('/'): This is a route decorator that tells Flask to associate the home() function with the URL path / (the root of the website).
- app.run(debug=True): Runs the Flask app with debugging enabled, so you can see detailed error messages.

- **Running the Application**: Save the code to a file (e.g., app.py), then run it from the terminal:

```bash
bash
```

```
python app.py
```

After running the command, open a browser and go to http://127.0.0.1:5000/. You should see "Hello, World!" displayed.

---

2. Routes, Templates, and Forms

Flask allows you to build dynamic web applications by handling multiple routes, rendering HTML templates, and processing forms.

- **Defining Multiple Routes**: A route in Flask is a URL path that triggers a function in your application. You can define multiple routes for different pages on your site.

```python
python
```

```python
@app.route('/about')
def about():
    return "This is the About page."
```

- **Rendering Templates**: Flask uses the Jinja2 template engine to render HTML templates. Templates are stored in the `templates` folder by default.
  - **Creating a Template**: Create a folder named `templates` in the same directory as your `app.py`. Inside this folder, create a file called `home.html`:

  ```
  html
  ```

  ```html
  <!DOCTYPE html>
  <html lang="en">
  <head>
      <meta charset="UTF-8">
      <meta              name="viewport"
  content="width=device-width,
  initial-scale=1.0">
      <title>Home Page</title>
  </head>
  ```

```
<body>
    <h1>Welcome   to   the   Home
Page!</h1>
    <p>Here  is  some  information
about the site.</p>
</body>
</html>
```

- o **Rendering the Template in Flask**: In your app.py, use the render_template() function to render the home.html template.

```
python

from flask import render_template

@app.route('/')
def home():
    return
render_template('home.html')
```

Flask will automatically look for the home.html file in the templates folder and render it when the / route is accessed.

- **Handling Forms**: Flask can process HTML forms using the request object to get data submitted by the user.
  - o **Form in HTML**:

```html
html
```

```html
<form                method="POST"
action="/submit">
    <input                type="text"
name="username"    placeholder="Enter
your username">
    <input                type="submit"
value="Submit">
</form>
```

o **Processing Form Data**: In your Flask application, you can use the `request.form` dictionary to access form data.

```python
python
```

```python
from flask import request

@app.route('/submit',
methods=['POST'])
def submit():
    username                =
request.form['username']
    return f"Hello, {username}!"
```

- **Explanation**:
    - The `method="POST"` attribute in the form sends the form data

to the server when the form is submitted.

- Flask handles the form submission using `request.form` and returns a personalized message to the user.

---

3. Working with Databases using SQLAlchemy

SQLAlchemy is a powerful Object Relational Mapper (ORM) used to interact with databases in Flask. It allows you to work with databases using Python objects rather than writing raw SQL queries.

- **Installing SQLAlchemy**: First, you need to install `Flask-SQLAlchemy` to work with databases in Flask:

bash

```
pip install flask_sqlalchemy
```

- **Setting Up the Database**: To use SQLAlchemy, you need to configure a database URL and create a database instance in your Flask application.

python

```
from flask_sqlalchemy import SQLAlchemy

app.config['SQLALCHEMY_DATABASE_URI']    =
'sqlite:///site.db'
db = SQLAlchemy(app)
```

- **Defining a Model**: SQLAlchemy models represent tables in your database. Define a model by creating a class that inherits from db.Model.

python

```
class Post(db.Model):
    id          =          db.Column(db.Integer,
primary_key=True)
    title    =    db.Column(db.String(100),
nullable=False)
    content      =        db.Column(db.Text,
nullable=False)
    date_posted  =   db.Column(db.DateTime,
default=datetime.utcnow)

    def __repr__(self):
        return        f"Post('{self.title}',
'{self.date_posted}')"
```

- o **Explanation**:

97

- db.Column: Defines a column in the table. The first argument is the column type (e.g., db.String, db.Integer), and you can specify properties such as nullable=False to require the field.
- default=datetime.utcnow: Sets the default value for the date_posted column to the current UTC time.

- **Creating the Database**: After defining the model, you can create the database by running:

```python
python
```

```python
from your_app import db
db.create_all()    # Creates all tables defined in models
```

- **Inserting Data into the Database**: You can create a new record by instantiating the model and adding it to the session.

```python
python
```

```python
@app.route('/add_post')
def add_post():
    post = Post(title='My First Post', content='This is the content of the post.')
    db.session.add(post)
```

```
db.session.commit()
return "Post added!"
```

- **Querying the Database**: To retrieve data from the database, use the `query` property.

```
python
```

```
@app.route('/posts')
def posts():
    posts = Post.query.all()   # Fetch all
posts
    return   render_template('posts.html',
posts=posts)
```

---

4. Project: Build a Simple Personal Blog

In this project, you'll build a simple personal blog using Flask and SQLAlchemy. The blog will allow you to create, view, and display posts.

- **Step 1: Define the Flask Application and Models**
  Create a new Flask application and define a `Post` model to store blog posts in the database.

```
python
```

```
from flask import Flask, render_template,
request, redirect, url_for
from flask_sqlalchemy import SQLAlchemy
from datetime import datetime

app = Flask(__name__)
app.config['SQLALCHEMY_DATABASE_URI']    =
'sqlite:///blog.db'
db = SQLAlchemy(app)

class Post(db.Model):
    id          =          db.Column(db.Integer,
primary_key=True)
    title    =    db.Column(db.String(100),
nullable=False)
    content       =          db.Column(db.Text,
nullable=False)
    date_posted  =   db.Column(db.DateTime,
default=datetime.utcnow)

    def __repr__(self):
        return         f"Post('{self.title}',
'{self.date_posted}')"
```

- **Step 2: Set Up Routes** Set up routes for displaying the homepage, creating a new post, and viewing posts.

python

```
@app.route('/')
```

```
def index():
    posts = Post.query.all()    # Get all
posts from the database
    return   render_template('index.html',
posts=posts)


@app.route('/add',           methods=['GET',
'POST'])
def add_post():
    if request.method == 'POST':
        title = request.form['title']
        content = request.form['content']
        new_post   =   Post(title=title,
content=content)
        db.session.add(new_post)
        db.session.commit()
        return redirect('/')
    return
render_template('add_post.html')
```

- **Step 3: Create Templates**
    - o **index.html**: Display a list of all blog posts.

```html
html

<h1>Blog Posts</h1>
{% for post in posts %}
    <h2>{{ post.title }}</h2>
    <p>{{ post.content }}</p>
    <small>{{ post.date_posted }}</small>
```

```
{% endfor %}
```

- o **add_post.html**: Create a form to add new blog posts.

html

```html
<h1>Add a New Post</h1>
<form method="POST">
    <label for="title">Title:</label>
    <input      type="text"      name="title"
required>
    <label for="content">Content:</label>
    <textarea                name="content"
required></textarea>
    <input type="submit" value="Add Post">
</form>
```

- **Step 4: Running the Application** Run the Flask application, navigate to `http://127.0.0.1:5000/` in your browser, and you should be able to view and add posts to your personal blog.

Conclusion:

In this chapter, you learned how to set up a basic Flask application, work with routes, templates, and forms, and interact with a database using SQLAlchemy. You applied these concepts to build a simple personal blog application. With Flask, you can now build dynamic web applications that can store and display data, providing a strong foundation for more advanced web development projects.

CHAPTER 9

DATA HANDLING WITH PANDAS AND NUMPY

Overview:

In this chapter, we will explore two of the most powerful libraries for data manipulation in Python: Pandas and NumPy. These libraries are essential for data analysis, providing tools to efficiently work with large datasets. Pandas offers robust data structures like DataFrames and Series for handling structured data, while NumPy provides powerful array operations for numerical data. You will learn how to leverage both libraries for tasks such as data cleaning, manipulation, and analysis. By the end of this chapter, you'll be able to work with real-world datasets and perform insightful analysis using Pandas and NumPy.

Topics Covered:

1. DataFrames, Series, and Operations in Pandas

Pandas is a high-level data manipulation library built on top of NumPy. It offers two primary data structures: Series and

DataFrames. Understanding how to work with these structures is essential for performing effective data manipulation.

- **Pandas Series**: A Series is a one-dimensional array-like object that can hold any data type (integers, floats, strings, etc.). It is similar to a list or array but with an associated index for each element.

  o **Creating a Series**:

  ```python
  import pandas as pd
  import numpy as np

  # Creating a simple Series
  s = pd.Series([1, 2, 3, 4, 5])
  print(s)
  ```

  o **Custom Index**: You can assign custom labels to the elements in a Series.

  ```python
  s = pd.Series([10, 20, 30],
  index=['a', 'b', 'c'])
  print(s)
  ```

- **Pandas DataFrame**: A DataFrame is a two-dimensional, labeled data structure similar to a table in a database or an

Excel spreadsheet. It is made up of rows and columns, where each column can hold different types of data.

- o **Creating a DataFrame**:

python

```python
data = {
    'Name': ['Alice', 'Bob',
'Charlie'],
    'Age': [25, 30, 35],
    'City': ['New York', 'Los
Angeles', 'Chicago']
}
```

```python
df = pd.DataFrame(data)
print(df)
```

- o **Accessing Data in a DataFrame**:
  - Accessing columns: `df['Age']` or `df.Age`
  - Accessing rows by index: `df.iloc[0]` (Access by index position)
  - Accessing rows by label: `df.loc[0]` (Access by label)
- o **Basic Operations on DataFrames**:
  - **Column Operations**:

python

```python
df['Age'] = df['Age'] + 1   #
Increment each value in the
'Age' column by 1
```

- **Row Operations**:

python

```python
df.loc[0] = ['Anna', 26,
'Boston']  # Modify a specific
row
```

- **Common DataFrame Operations**:
  - **Sorting**: df.sort_values(by='Age')
  - **Filtering**: df[df['Age'] > 30]
  - **Summary Statistics**: df.describe()

---

2. Numpy Arrays and Vectorized Operations

NumPy is a fundamental package for numerical computing in Python. It provides a powerful array object and a variety of mathematical functions to manipulate large datasets.

- **Creating NumPy Arrays**: NumPy arrays are more efficient than Python lists for handling numerical data. They are the core data structure of NumPy.
  - **Creating a NumPy Array**:

```python
python

import numpy as np

arr = np.array([1, 2, 3, 4, 5])
print(arr)
```

o **Array Operations**: NumPy supports vectorized operations, which means you can perform element-wise operations without needing explicit loops. This significantly improves performance.

```python
python

arr = np.array([1, 2, 3, 4, 5])
arr = arr * 2    # Element-wise
multiplication
print(arr)   # Output: [2, 4, 6, 8,
10]
```

- **Broadcasting**: NumPy arrays support broadcasting, allowing you to perform operations on arrays of different shapes.

```python
python

arr1 = np.array([1, 2, 3])
arr2 = np.array([4, 5, 6])
```

```
result = arr1 + arr2     # Element-wise
addition
print(result)   # Output: [5, 7, 9]
```

- **Array Operations with Pandas DataFrames**: You can combine NumPy arrays with Pandas DataFrames for efficient data manipulation. For example, you can perform element-wise operations on entire DataFrame columns using NumPy arrays:

```python
python
```

```python
df['Age'] = np.log(df['Age'])     # Apply
NumPy logarithm to the 'Age' column
```

---

3. Data Cleaning and Manipulation

Data cleaning is one of the most important steps in the data analysis pipeline. Pandas provides a wide array of functions to handle missing data, duplicates, and other data issues.

- **Handling Missing Data**: Pandas has built-in methods to handle missing values (represented by NaN in Python).
  - **Detecting Missing Data**:

    ```python
    python
    ```

```
df.isnull()  # Returns a DataFrame of
the same shape with True/False for
NaN values
```

- o **Filling Missing Data**: You can fill missing values with a specific value, forward-fill, or backward-fill.

```python
python
```

```
df.fillna(0)    # Replace missing
values with 0
```

- o **Dropping Missing Data**: You can drop rows or columns with missing data.

```python
python
```

```
df.dropna()  # Drop rows with any
missing values
```

- **Handling Duplicates**: Pandas allows you to identify and remove duplicate entries.

```python
python
```

```
df.drop_duplicates()    # Remove duplicate
rows
```

- **Changing Data Types**: You can change the data type of a column using the `astype()` method.

python

```
df['Age'] = df['Age'].astype(float)    #
Convert 'Age' column to float
```

- **Applying Functions to Data**: You can use the `apply()` method to apply custom functions to rows or columns.

python

```
df['Age'] = df['Age'].apply(lambda x: x +
1)   # Add 1 to each value in the 'Age'
column
```

4. Project: Analyze a Dataset (e.g., Stock Data)

In this project, we will analyze a stock dataset to perform some common data analysis tasks such as calculating the moving average, filtering data, and visualizing trends.

- **Step 1: Importing the Dataset** For this project, we'll use a CSV file containing stock price data. You can download a sample dataset from online resources or use a publicly available stock data API like Yahoo Finance.
  - o **Loading the Data**:

111

```
python
```

```
df = pd.read_csv('stock_data.csv')
print(df.head())  # Display the first
5 rows
```

- **Step 2: Data Cleaning** Before analyzing the data, ensure that any missing or duplicate values are handled.

```
python
```

```
df.dropna(inplace=True)  # Remove rows with
missing data
df.drop_duplicates(inplace=True)   # Remove
duplicate rows
```

- **Step 3: Calculating the Moving Average** A moving average is a common way to analyze stock trends. Let's calculate a simple 5-day moving average.

```
python
```

```
df['5-day            MA']                 =
df['Close'].rolling(window=5).mean()
print(df[['Date',    'Close',    '5-day
MA']].head(10))
```

- **Step 4: Filtering Data** You can filter stock data based on certain criteria. For example, filtering data to only show stocks where the closing price is greater than $100.

python

```
filtered_df = df[df['Close'] > 100]
print(filtered_df.head())
```

- **Step 5: Visualizing the Data** Use `matplotlib` to create visualizations of the stock price trends.

python

```
import matplotlib.pyplot as plt

plt.plot(df['Date'],              df['Close'],
label='Close Price')
plt.plot(df['Date'],    df['5-day    MA'],
label='5-day Moving Average')
plt.xlabel('Date')
plt.ylabel('Price')
plt.title('Stock    Price    and    Moving
Average')
plt.legend()
plt.show()
```

This will produce a line graph showing the stock's closing price and its moving average over time.

Conclusion:

In this chapter, we learned how to efficiently handle and manipulate data using Pandas and NumPy. We covered the essentials of Pandas DataFrames and Series, NumPy arrays, and vectorized operations for fast numerical computations. We also discussed data cleaning techniques, including handling missing values, duplicates, and data type conversions. Finally, you applied these skills in a project to analyze stock data, including calculating moving averages, filtering data, and visualizing trends. With these tools, you are now equipped to work with real-world datasets and perform powerful data analysis in Python.

CHAPTER 10

INTRODUCTION TO DATABASES WITH SQLITE

Overview:

In this chapter, we will introduce you to using databases in Python, with a focus on SQLite. SQLite is a lightweight, serverless database that is perfect for small to medium-sized applications. It is embedded within the Python standard library and provides a simple yet powerful way to manage data. We will cover how to set up a SQLite database, perform basic CRUD (Create, Read, Update, Delete) operations, and use SQLAlchemy for more advanced database management. By the end of this chapter, you will have built a simple contact management system using SQLite and SQLAlchemy.

Topics Covered:

1. Setting Up a Database with SQLite

SQLite is an embedded database engine that stores data in a single file on the local filesystem. It is ideal for applications that require a simple, self-contained database without the need for a server.

- **Installing SQLite**: SQLite is included with Python by default, so you do not need to install it separately. You can use the `sqlite3` module, which is part of the Python standard library.

- **Creating a Database**: To create a new SQLite database, you simply need to connect to a file. If the file doesn't exist, SQLite will create it for you.

```python
import sqlite3

# Connect to a database (or create it if it
doesn't exist)
conn = sqlite3.connect('contacts.db')

# Create a cursor object to interact with
the database
cursor = conn.cursor()
```

- **Creating a Table**: After creating a connection to the database, you can create tables to store your data. A table is created using the CREATE TABLE SQL statement.

```python
cursor.execute('''CREATE    TABLE    IF    NOT
EXISTS contacts (
```

```
           id   INTEGER   PRIMARY
KEY,
           name TEXT NOT NULL,
           phone TEXT NOT NULL,
           email TEXT)''')


# Commit the changes and close the
connection
conn.commit()
```

---

2. Performing CRUD Operations (Create, Read, Update, Delete)

CRUD operations are the basic actions used in database management. Let's explore each of these operations in the context of SQLite.

- **Create (Insert Data)**: The INSERT INTO SQL statement is used to add new rows to a table.

```
python

cursor.execute('''INSERT   INTO   contacts
(name, phone, email)
                 VALUES  (?,  ?,  ?)''',
('Alice',               '123-456-7890',
'alice@example.com'))


# Commit the changes to the database
conn.commit()
```

- **Read (Query Data)**: You can retrieve data using the SELECT statement. You can fetch all rows or just a specific set of rows using WHERE clauses.

python

```
cursor.execute('SELECT * FROM contacts')
rows = cursor.fetchall()  # Fetch all rows
for row in rows:
    print(row)   # Each row is a tuple
containing column values

# Fetching specific contact by name
cursor.execute('SELECT  *  FROM  contacts
WHERE name = ?', ('Alice',))
result = cursor.fetchone()  # Fetch one row
print(result)
```

- **Update (Modify Data)**: You can modify existing data using the UPDATE statement.

python

```
cursor.execute('''UPDATE contacts
                SET phone = ?
                WHERE  name  =  ?''',
('987-654-3210', 'Alice'))
conn.commit()
```

- **Delete (Remove Data)**: The `DELETE FROM` statement allows you to delete rows from a table.

python

```
cursor.execute('DELETE FROM contacts WHERE
name = ?', ('Alice',))
conn.commit()
```

3. Using SQLAlchemy for Database Management

SQLAlchemy is an ORM (Object Relational Mapper) for Python, which allows you to interact with databases using Python objects rather than writing raw SQL queries. It makes database management easier and more Pythonic, especially for larger applications.

- **Installing SQLAlchemy**: To use SQLAlchemy, you need to install it first:

bash

```
pip install sqlalchemy
```

- **Setting Up SQLAlchemy with SQLite**: SQLAlchemy uses a declarative syntax to define the structure of your database tables as Python classes. You can connect to the SQLite database using the `create_engine()` function.

119

```python
python

from sqlalchemy import create_engine,
Column, Integer, String
from sqlalchemy.ext.declarative import
declarative_base
from sqlalchemy.orm import sessionmaker

# Define the base class for all models
Base = declarative_base()

# Define the Contact class (model)
class Contact(Base):
    __tablename__ = 'contacts'

    id = Column(Integer, primary_key=True)
    name = Column(String, nullable=False)
    phone = Column(String, nullable=False)
    email = Column(String)

# Create an SQLite database and engine
engine                               =
create_engine('sqlite:///contacts.db')

# Create the table in the database (if it
doesn't exist)
Base.metadata.create_all(engine)
```

```
# Create a session to interact with the
database
Session = sessionmaker(bind=engine)
session = Session()
```

- **Performing CRUD Operations with SQLAlchemy**: With SQLAlchemy, you can easily create, read, update, and delete data using Python objects.

  o **Create (Add a Contact)**:

    python

    ```
    new_contact = Contact(name='Bob',
    phone='555-555-5555',
    email='bob@example.com')
    session.add(new_contact)
    session.commit()
    ```

  o **Read (Query a Contact)**:

    python

    ```
    contact =
    session.query(Contact).filter_by(na
    me='Bob').first()
    print(contact.name, contact.phone,
    contact.email)
    ```

  o **Update (Modify a Contact)**:

```python

contact                              =
session.query(Contact).filter_by(na
me='Bob').first()
contact.phone = '555-999-9999'
session.commit()
```

- o **Delete (Remove a Contact):**

```python

contact                              =
session.query(Contact).filter_by(na
me='Bob').first()
session.delete(contact)
session.commit()
```

---

4. Project: Build a Contact Management System

In this project, we will use SQLite and SQLAlchemy to build a simple contact management system. The system will allow you to:

- Add new contacts.
- View all contacts.
- Update existing contacts.
- Delete contacts.

- **Step 1: Define the Contact Model (SQLAlchemy)**: First, we define the `Contact` class as shown earlier, using SQLAlchemy to model the contact information.

- **Step 2: Create Functions for CRUD Operations**: We will define functions for adding, viewing, updating, and deleting contacts.

python

```python
def add_contact(name, phone, email):
    contact      =      Contact(name=name,
phone=phone, email=email)
    session.add(contact)
    session.commit()
    print(f"Contact      {name}      added
successfully!")


def view_contacts():
    contacts                          =
session.query(Contact).all()
    for contact in contacts:
        print(f"{contact.name},
{contact.phone}, {contact.email}")


def    update_contact(name,      new_phone,
new_email):
    contact                          =
session.query(Contact).filter_by(name=nam
e).first()
```

```
        if contact:
            contact.phone = new_phone
            contact.email = new_email
            session.commit()
            print(f"Contact      {name}      updated
successfully!")
        else:
            print(f"Contact       {name}       not
found!")


def delete_contact(name):
    contact                                     =
session.query(Contact).filter_by(name=nam
e).first()
        if contact:
            session.delete(contact)
            session.commit()
            print(f"Contact     {name}     deleted
successfully!")
        else:
            print(f"Contact       {name}       not
found!")
```

- **Step 3: User Interface**: To interact with the system, you can create a simple user interface using the command line. Here's how to add, view, update, and delete contacts:

```python
python
```

```python
def main():
    while True:
        print("\nContact          Management
System")
        print("1. Add Contact")
        print("2. View Contacts")
        print("3. Update Contact")
        print("4. Delete Contact")
        print("5. Exit")

        choice = input("Enter your choice:
")

        if choice == '1':
            name = input("Enter name: ")
            phone = input("Enter phone: ")
            email = input("Enter email: ")
            add_contact(name,       phone,
email)
        elif choice == '2':
            view_contacts()
        elif choice == '3':
            name = input("Enter the name of
the contact to update: ")
            new_phone = input("Enter  new
phone: ")
            new_email = input("Enter  new
email: ")
```

```
                update_contact(name,
new_phone, new_email)
        elif choice == '4':
            name = input("Enter the name of
the contact to delete: ")
            delete_contact(name)
        elif choice == '5':
            print("Goodbye!")
            break
        else:
            print("Invalid choice! Please
try again.")

if __name__ == "__main__":
    main()
```

Conclusion:

In this chapter, we learned how to work with databases using SQLite in Python. You set up a simple SQLite database, performed CRUD operations, and explored how to use SQLAlchemy to interact with the database using Python objects. You also applied your knowledge to build a simple contact management system, allowing you to add, view, update, and delete contact information. With these skills, you can now integrate databases into your Python applications and manage data more effectively.

CHAPTER 11

BUILDING COMMAND-LINE APPLICATIONS WITH PYTHON

Overview:

Command-line applications are a powerful and efficient way to interact with programs directly through the terminal. In this chapter, we'll explore how to build useful command-line applications in Python. We will cover how to parse command-line arguments, build reusable command-line scripts, and automate tasks with Python. By the end of the chapter, you will have a practical project—a file organizer command-line application—that you can use to streamline file management on your computer.

Topics Covered:

1. Parsing Command-Line Arguments with argparse

Command-line arguments are parameters passed to a script when executed from the terminal. Python provides the `argparse` module to easily handle these arguments and create user-friendly CLI applications.

- **Setting Up argparse**: To use `argparse`, you first need to import the module and create a parser object. Then, you define the expected command-line arguments.

```python

import argparse

# Create a parser object
parser                                    =
argparse.ArgumentParser(description="A
simple command-line app")

# Add arguments to the parser
parser.add_argument('name',        type=str,
help='Your name')
parser.add_argument('-a',             '--age',
type=int, help='Your age', default=30)

# Parse the arguments
args = parser.parse_args()

print(f"Hello, {args.name}!")
print(f"Age: {args.age}")
```

- **Command-Line Usage**: To run the script, you would execute it from the terminal like this:

```bash
```

```
python script.py Alice --age 25
```

Output:

```
makefile
```

```
Hello, Alice!
Age: 25
```

- **Positional and Optional Arguments**:
    - **Positional Arguments**: These are required arguments that must appear in the specified order. In the example above, `name` is a positional argument.
    - **Optional Arguments**: These are arguments that are optional and can be specified with flags. For example, `-a` or `--age` is an optional argument.
- **Argument Types and Default Values**: You can specify the expected type for each argument, and set default values for optional arguments.

```
python
```

```
parser.add_argument('--verbose',
action='store_true', help='Enable verbose
mode')
```

- **Custom Help Messages**: The `argparse` module automatically generates help messages for your script. You can see this help message by running the following:

```bash
python script.py --help
```

---

2. Building Reusable Command-Line Scripts

Once you have basic argument parsing in place, it's important to structure your Python scripts in a way that they can be reused for various tasks or with different sets of arguments. The idea is to encapsulate the functionality into functions and call them as needed based on the command-line arguments.

- **Encapsulating Logic in Functions**: Organizing your code into functions allows for better reusability and modularity. Here's an example:

```python
import argparse

def greet_user(name, age):
    print(f"Hello, {name}!")
    print(f"Age: {age}")
```

```python
def main():
    parser                          =
argparse.ArgumentParser(description="Gree
t the user")
    parser.add_argument('name', type=str,
help='Your name')
    parser.add_argument('-a',      '--age',
type=int, help='Your age', default=30)
    args = parser.parse_args()

    greet_user(args.name, args.age)

if __name__ == '__main__':
    main()
```

This structure allows you to reuse the `greet_user` function in other contexts if needed.

- **Command-Line Argument Validation**: It's important to validate user inputs, especially if you're dealing with user-generated data like file paths or numerical values. You can use conditions or custom functions to check if arguments meet certain requirements.

```python
python

parser.add_argument('number',      type=int,
help='A number')
args = parser.parse_args()
```

```
if args.number < 0:
    print("Error:  Number  must  be  non-
negative.")
```

---

3. Automating Tasks with Python

One of the most powerful features of command-line applications is task automation. Python allows you to automate repetitive tasks like file renaming, backups, or data processing with minimal code.

- **Automating File Management**: Python's `os` and `shutil` modules are great for automating file-related tasks such as moving, renaming, or deleting files.

    o **Renaming Files**:

    ```
    python
    ```

    ```
    import os
    ```

    ```
    def rename_file(old_name, new_name):
        os.rename(old_name, new_name)
        print(f"File      renamed      from
    {old_name} to {new_name}")
    ```

    o **Moving Files**:

    ```
    python
    ```

```
import shutil

def move_file(source, destination):
    shutil.move(source, destination)
    print(f"File        moved        to
{destination}")
```

  o **Deleting Files**:

```
python
```

```
def delete_file(file_path):
    os.remove(file_path)
    print(f"File          {file_path}
deleted.")
```

- **Scheduling Tasks**: You can automate periodic tasks by integrating Python with task schedulers like `cron` (on Linux) or Task Scheduler (on Windows). Alternatively, you can use the `schedule` library to run tasks at specific intervals in your script.

  o Example using the `schedule` library to run a task every minute:

```
python
```

```
import schedule
import time
```

```
def job():
    print("Running          scheduled
task...")


schedule.every(1).minute.do(job)

while True:
    schedule.run_pending()
    time.sleep(1)
```

---

4. Project: Build a File Organizer CLI App

In this project, you'll build a simple file organizer CLI app that automates the task of organizing files in a specified directory based on their file extensions. This app will allow you to categorize files into folders (e.g., images, documents, audio, etc.) based on their type.

- **Step 1: Define the Structure** We will use the os and shutil modules to handle file management and organize files based on their extensions.
- **Step 2: Define File Types**: First, create a dictionary that maps file extensions to categories:

python

```
file_types = {
```

```python
    'images': ['.jpg', '.jpeg', '.png',
'.gif'],
    'documents': ['.pdf', '.txt', '.docx',
'.xlsx'],
    'audio': ['.mp3', '.wav', '.flac'],
    'videos': ['.mp4', '.avi', '.mkv'],
    'others': []
}
```

- **Step 3: Organize Files**: Write a function to organize files based on their extensions:

```python
python

import os
import shutil

def organize_files(directory):
    for filename in os.listdir(directory):
        file_path                        =
os.path.join(directory, filename)
        if os.path.isfile(file_path):
            ext                          =
os.path.splitext(filename)[1].lower()
            target_folder = 'others'    #
Default category

            for category, extensions in
file_types.items():
                if ext in extensions:
```

```
            target_folder        =
category

            break


        target_folder_path        =
os.path.join(directory, target_folder)
            if                not
os.path.exists(target_folder_path):

os.makedirs(target_folder_path)


        shutil.move(file_path,
os.path.join(target_folder_path,
filename))
        print(f"Moved:  {filename}  to
{target_folder}/")
```

- **Step 4: Command-Line Interface**: Use `argparse` to create a command-line interface for the app:

```python
import argparse

def main():
    parser                =
argparse.ArgumentParser(description="Orga
nize files in a directory.")
    parser.add_argument('directory',
type=str, help='Directory to organize')
```

```
args = parser.parse_args()

organize_files(args.directory)

if __name__ == '__main__':
    main()
```

- **Step 5: Run the App**: To run the file organizer, execute the following command in your terminal:

```bash
python                    file_organizer.py
/path/to/your/directory
```

The app will organize all files in the specified directory into subfolders based on their extensions.

Conclusion:

In this chapter, you learned how to build command-line applications in Python using the `argparse` module. We covered parsing command-line arguments, building reusable scripts, and automating tasks with Python. You also applied these skills to create a practical project—a file organizer CLI app—that helps automate the task of organizing files based on their extensions. Command-line applications are a powerful way to interact with programs and automate repetitive tasks, and with Python, you have a robust set of tools to create efficient, user-friendly applications.

CHAPTER 12

INTRODUCTION TO GUI DEVELOPMENT WITH TKINTER

Overview:

Graphical User Interfaces (GUIs) allow users to interact with applications through graphical elements such as buttons, text fields, and labels, making software more user-friendly. Tkinter is the standard GUI library for Python and provides all the tools you need to create desktop applications. In this chapter, we'll explore how to build simple GUIs using Tkinter. You will learn about basic Tkinter widgets, event-driven programming, and layout management. By the end of this chapter, you will have created a simple calculator app using Tkinter, reinforcing your understanding of GUI development in Python.

Topics Covered:

1. Basic Tkinter Widgets: Buttons, Labels, and Text Fields

Tkinter provides various widgets to create graphical components in your application. Some of the most commonly used widgets are buttons, labels, and text fields.

- **Creating a Tkinter Window**: To create a Tkinter application, you first need to initialize the main window using the `Tk()` class.

python

```
import tkinter as tk

# Create the main window
root = tk.Tk()

# Set the window title
root.title("Simple Tkinter App")

# Run the Tkinter event loop
root.mainloop()
```

- **Labels**: Labels are used to display text or images on the window. You can create a label by using the `Label` widget.

python

```
label = tk.Label(root, text="Welcome to Tkinter!")
label.pack()  # Pack the widget into the window
```

140

- o **Customizing Labels**: You can change the font, color, and alignment of the text in a label.

python

```
label = tk.Label(root, text="Hello,
World!",    font=("Arial",    14),
fg="blue")
label.pack()
```

- **Buttons**: Buttons allow users to trigger actions when clicked. You can create a button using the `Button` widget.

python

```
button = tk.Button(root, text="Click Me",
command=lambda: print("Button clicked!"))
button.pack()
```

- o **Command Callback**: The `command` parameter specifies the function that should be called when the button is clicked.
- **Text Fields (Entry Widgets)**: Entry widgets allow users to input text. You can create an entry field using the `Entry` widget.

python

```
entry = tk.Entry(root)
entry.pack()
```

- o **Getting Input from the Entry Widget**: To retrieve the text entered in the entry field, use the `get()` method.

  python

  ```
  user_input = entry.get()
  print(f"You entered: {user_input}")
  ```

---

2. Event-Driven Programming with Tkinter

Tkinter is event-driven, meaning the application reacts to user interactions such as button clicks, key presses, and mouse movements. You can define what should happen when a specific event occurs by binding functions to these events.

- **Binding Functions to Events**: Tkinter allows you to bind events to widgets. For example, you can define a function that will execute when a button is clicked.

  python

  ```
  def on_button_click():
      print("Button clicked!")
  ```

```
button = tk.Button(root, text="Click Me",
command=on_button_click)
button.pack()
```

You can also bind events to other widgets or even the window itself.

```
python
```

```
def on_key_press(event):
    print(f"Key pressed: {event.char}")
```

```
root.bind("<KeyPress>", on_key_press)    #
Bind key press event to the window
```

- **Common Events in Tkinter**:
  - Mouse Events: `<Button-1>` (left click), `<Button-2>` (middle click), `<Button-3>` (right click).
  - Keyboard Events: `<KeyPress>` and `<KeyRelease>`.
  - Window Events: `<Configure>`, `<Close>`, etc.

---

3. Organizing Layouts with Tkinter's Grid and Pack Methods

Tkinter provides two main methods for organizing widgets inside the window: the `pack()` and `grid()` methods.

- **Using `pack()` for Layout**: The `pack()` method arranges widgets vertically or horizontally within the window. You can customize the alignment and order of widgets using the `side`, `fill`, and `expand` options.

python

```
label = tk.Label(root, text="This is a
label")
label.pack(side=tk.TOP, fill=tk.X)
```

  o **Packing Widgets**:
    - `side=tk.TOP`: Pack the widget at the top of the window.
    - `fill=tk.X`: Fill the width of the window.

- **Using `grid()` for Layout**: The `grid()` method is used to create a more complex layout with rows and columns, similar to a table or spreadsheet.

python

```
label1 = tk.Label(root, text="Label 1")
label1.grid(row=0, column=0)   # Place the
label in the first row and column

label2 = tk.Label(root, text="Label 2")
```

144

```
label2.grid(row=0, column=1)  # Place the
label in the first row, second column
```

- o **Customizing Grid Layout**: You can specify the row and column span, and control the widget's alignment and resizing behavior.

  python

  ```
  button = tk.Button(root, text="Click
  Me")
  button.grid(row=1,          column=0,
  columnspan=2, sticky="ew")  # Expand
  button across columns
  ```

- **Choosing Between `pack()` and `grid()`**:
  - o Use `pack()` when you need a simple, linear arrangement of widgets.
  - o Use `grid()` when you need more control over the positioning of widgets, such as in a table-like layout.

4. Project: Build a Simple Calculator App

Now that we've covered the basics of Tkinter, let's build a simple calculator app. The app will have buttons for digits and basic operations (addition, subtraction, multiplication, and division), and a display to show the result.

- **Step 1: Define the Tkinter Window and Layout** First, create the main window and the basic layout using grid() to arrange the calculator's buttons and the display.

python

```python
import tkinter as tk

# Create the main window
root = tk.Tk()
root.title("Calculator")

# Entry widget to display the result
display    =    tk.Entry(root,    width=16,
font=("Arial",    24),    borderwidth=2,
relief="solid", justify="right")
display.grid(row=0,              column=0,
columnspan=4)

# Function to update the display with
button clicks
def button_click(value):
    current = display.get()
    display.delete(0, tk.END)
```

```
display.insert(tk.END,      current      +
value)
```

- **Step 2: Define Button Functions** Each button will update the display or perform a calculation when clicked.

python

```python
# Button functions
def calculate():
    try:
        result = eval(display.get())    #
Evaluate the expression from the display
        display.delete(0, tk.END)
        display.insert(tk.END,
str(result))
    except Exception as e:
        display.delete(0, tk.END)
        display.insert(tk.END, "Error")

def clear():
    display.delete(0, tk.END)  # Clear the
display
```

- **Step 3: Create Buttons for Digits and Operations** Define buttons for the digits (0-9) and operations (+, -, *, /).

python

147

```python
# Create the calculator buttons
buttons = [
    ('7', 1, 0), ('8', 1, 1), ('9', 1, 2),
('/', 1, 3),
    ('4', 2, 0), ('5', 2, 1), ('6', 2, 2),
('*', 2, 3),
    ('1', 3, 0), ('2', 3, 1), ('3', 3, 2),
('-', 3, 3),
    ('0', 4, 0), ('C', 4, 1), ('=', 4, 2),
('+', 4, 3),
]

for (text, row, column) in buttons:
    if text == "=":
        button      =       tk.Button(root,
text=text,          width=10,          height=3,
font=("Arial", 18), command=calculate)
    elif text == "C":
        button      =       tk.Button(root,
text=text,          width=10,          height=3,
font=("Arial", 18), command=clear)
    else:
        button      =       tk.Button(root,
text=text,          width=10,          height=3,
font=("Arial",      18),      command=lambda
value=text: button_click(value))

    button.grid(row=row, column=column)
```

```
# Run the Tkinter event loop
root.mainloop()
```

- **Step 4: Run the Application** Run the app by executing the Python script, and you should see a simple calculator with a display and buttons for digits and operations. When you click the buttons, the display will update, and calculations will be performed when you click =.

Conclusion:

In this chapter, you learned how to build graphical user interfaces (GUIs) using Tkinter. We covered the basics of Tkinter widgets, such as buttons, labels, and text fields, and explored event-driven programming, where your app responds to user interactions. We also learned how to organize layouts using Tkinter's `pack()` and `grid()` methods. Finally, you applied these skills to build a simple calculator app, demonstrating how to handle user input and perform calculations in a GUI-based application. Tkinter is a great tool for creating desktop applications, and with these fundamentals, you can start building more advanced applications with graphical interfaces.

CHAPTER 13

INTRODUCTION TO APIS AND WEB SERVICES

Overview:

In this chapter, we'll explore APIs (Application Programming Interfaces) and how they allow applications to interact with external services over the web. We will focus on using Python to send HTTP requests, work with JSON data returned from APIs, and handle authentication. By the end of this chapter, you will have built an app that fetches data from a public API, helping you understand how APIs work and how to integrate them into your Python applications.

Topics Covered:

1. Sending HTTP Requests with `requests`

To work with APIs in Python, we need a way to send HTTP requests. The `requests` library is a popular and easy-to-use HTTP library that allows you to send HTTP requests and handle responses.

- **Installing the `requests` Library**: First, install the `requests` library using pip:

```bash
bash
```

```bash
pip install requests
```

- **Sending a GET Request**: The most common way to interact with APIs is by sending a GET request, which retrieves data from a server.

```python
python
```

```python
import requests

url = "https://api.example.com/data"
response = requests.get(url)

# Check the status code to ensure the
request was successful
if response.status_code == 200:
    print("Request successful")
    data = response.json()  # Convert JSON
response to Python dictionary
    print(data)
else:
    print(f"Request failed with status
code {response.status_code}")
```

- o **Explanation**:
    - ▪ `requests.get(url)` sends a GET request to the specified URL.
    - ▪ `response.status_code` checks the HTTP status code of the response (e.g., 200 for success).
    - ▪ `response.json()` converts the JSON data returned by the API into a Python dictionary.
- **Sending a POST Request**: In addition to GET requests, you can also send POST requests, often used to send data to an API.

```python
url = "https://api.example.com/submit"
data = {"name": "Alice", "age": 30}
response = requests.post(url, json=data)

if response.status_code == 200:
    print("Data submitted successfully")
```

---

2. Working with JSON Data from APIs

APIs commonly return data in the JSON (JavaScript Object Notation) format, which is easy to read and work with in Python.

The `requests` library makes it simple to work with JSON data by providing the `json()` method.

- **Parsing JSON Data**: Once you have received the data, you can parse it into Python dictionaries and work with it like any other Python object.

```python
import requests

url = "https://jsonplaceholder.typicode.com/todos/1"
response = requests.get(url)

# Parse JSON data
todo = response.json()
print(todo)

# Accessing specific values from the JSON object
print(f"Title: {todo['title']}")
print(f"Completed: {todo['completed']}")
```

  o **Explanation**:
    - The API returns a dictionary-like object, and you can access values using keys,

just like working with a standard Python dictionary.

- **Handling Nested JSON Data**: Many APIs return nested JSON objects. To handle nested data, you can access sub-dictionaries using their keys.

```python
python
```

```python
url                                    =
"https://jsonplaceholder.typicode.com/use
rs/1"
response = requests.get(url)
user = response.json()

# Accessing nested data
print(f"User Name: {user['name']}")
print(f"Company:
{user['company']['name']}")
```

- o **Explanation**:
  - You can access nested data by chaining key accesses. In this example, the company data is nested inside the company key.

3. Authentication and API Keys

Many APIs require authentication to ensure that only authorized users can access the data or perform certain actions. One common method of authentication is using API keys.

- **Using API Keys**: API keys are typically passed as a parameter in the request headers or as part of the URL.

```python
python

import requests

url = "https://api.example.com/data"
headers = {
    "Authorization": "Bearer YOUR_API_KEY"
}

response        =        requests.get(url,
headers=headers)

if response.status_code == 200:
    print("Data fetched successfully")
    data = response.json()
    print(data)
else:
    print(f"Failed    to    fetch    data:
{response.status_code}")
```

- o **Explanation**:
  - In the `Authorization` header, you provide your API key (replacing `YOUR_API_KEY` with your actual key).
  - The `Bearer` token type is commonly used, but some APIs may require a different method of passing the key.
- **Environment Variables for Security**: To avoid hardcoding your API key in the code, store it in an environment variable.

```python
import os
import requests

api_key = os.getenv('API_KEY')   # Get the
API key from environment variable
url = "https://api.example.com/data"
headers = {
    "Authorization": f"Bearer {api_key}"
}

response          =          requests.get(url,
headers=headers)
```

- o **Explanation**:

156

- Using `os.getenv()` allows you to retrieve the API key from an environment variable, keeping sensitive information out of your source code.

---

4. Project: Build an App That Fetches Data from a Public API

In this project, you'll build a simple app that fetches data from a public API and displays it. We'll use the JSONPlaceholder, a free API that provides fake data for testing.

- **Step 1: Set Up the Application** We will fetch a list of users from the API and display their information.

python

```python
import requests

def fetch_users():
    url = "https://jsonplaceholder.typicode.com/users"
    response = requests.get(url)
    if response.status_code == 200:
        users = response.json()
        return users
    else:
        print("Failed to fetch users")
```

```
        return []

def display_users(users):
    for user in users:
        print(f"Name: {user['name']}")
        print(f"Email: {user['email']}")
        print(f"Phone: {user['phone']}")
        print("-" * 40)

if __name__ == "__main__":
    users = fetch_users()
    if users:
        display_users(users)
```

- o **Explanation**:
  - The `fetch_users()` function sends a GET request to the API and retrieves a list of users.
  - The `display_users()` function prints the name, email, and phone of each user.
- **Step 2: Run the Application** When you run the script, it fetches data from the API and displays the list of users.

```makefile

Name: Leanne Graham
Email: Sincere@april.biz
Phone: 1-770-736-8031 x56442
------------------------------------------
```

```
Name: Ervin Howell
Email: Shanna@melissa.tv
Phone: 010-692-6593 x09125
-----------------------------------------
```

- **Step 3: Add Error Handling and API Key (Optional)**
  To make the app more robust, you can add error handling
  and use an API key if required by the API. You can also
  extend the functionality to display specific user details or
  integrate additional API features.

Conclusion:

In this chapter, you learned how to interact with APIs in Python
using the `requests` library. You explored sending HTTP
requests, working with JSON data, handling authentication with
API keys, and built a project to fetch and display data from a
public API. APIs are integral to modern web applications, and
understanding how to integrate them into your Python projects
opens up endless possibilities for fetching and processing data
from the web.

CHAPTER 14

WORKING WITH JSON AND XML DATA

Overview:

In this chapter, we will explore how to handle JSON (JavaScript Object Notation) and XML (eXtensible Markup Language) data in Python. Both formats are widely used for data exchange between systems, APIs, and applications. Python provides built-in libraries to parse, generate, and manipulate both JSON and XML data. You will learn how to convert between these formats and build a practical project: a JSON-to-XML converter.

Topics Covered:

1. Parsing and Generating JSON

JSON is a lightweight data-interchange format that is easy for humans to read and write and easy for machines to parse and generate. Python's `json` module provides a simple way to work with JSON data.

- **Parsing JSON Data**: To parse JSON data (convert JSON into Python objects), use the `json.loads()` function. This function takes a JSON string and converts it into a Python dictionary.

```python
import json

json_data = '{"name": "Alice", "age": 30, "city": "New York"}'

# Parse JSON string into Python dictionary
data = json.loads(json_data)

print(data)
print(data['name'])  # Output: Alice
```

  o **Explanation**:
    - `json.loads()` converts a JSON-formatted string into a Python dictionary.
    - The dictionary is then accessed using standard Python syntax.
- **Generating JSON Data**: To generate JSON data (convert Python objects into JSON format), use the `json.dumps()` function. This function takes a Python object and converts it into a JSON string.

161

```python
python

import json

python_data = {'name': 'Bob', 'age': 25,
'city': 'Los Angeles'}

# Convert Python dictionary to JSON string
json_data = json.dumps(python_data)

print(json_data)
```

- o **Explanation**:
  - `json.dumps()` converts a Python object into a JSON-formatted string.
  - The result is a string that can be written to a file, sent over a network, or processed further.
- **Writing JSON to a File**: You can easily write JSON data to a file using the `json.dump()` function, which is similar to `json.dumps()`, but it writes directly to a file.

```python
python

import json

data = {'name': 'Charlie', 'age': 28,
'city': 'Chicago'}
```

```
with open('data.json', 'w') as file:
    json.dump(data, file)  # Write JSON to
a file
```

- o **Explanation**:
  - ▪ `json.dump()` writes the JSON object to a file. The `file` object must be opened in write mode.
- **Reading JSON from a File**: To read JSON data from a file and convert it into a Python object, use the `json.load()` function.

python

```
import json

with open('data.json', 'r') as file:
    data = json.load(file)   # Load JSON
data from a file

print(data)
```

---

2. Working with XML Data Using `xml.etree.ElementTree`

XML is another widely used data format, especially in legacy systems and web services. Python provides the `xml.etree.ElementTree` module to parse, generate, and manipulate XML data.

163

- **Parsing XML Data**: To parse XML data, use the `ElementTree` class from the `xml.etree.ElementTree` module. The `fromstring()` function parses an XML string into an element tree.

python

```python
import xml.etree.ElementTree as ET

xml_data = '''<person>
                <name>Alice</name>
                <age>30</age>
                <city>New York</city>
            </person>'''

# Parse XML string into an ElementTree
object
root = ET.fromstring(xml_data)

# Access elements using their tag names
print(root.find('name').text)   # Output:
Alice
print(root.find('age').text)   # Output: 30
```

  o **Explanation**:
    - `ET.fromstring()` converts an XML string into an element tree structure.

164

- You can access individual elements using the `.find()` method, specifying the tag name.

- **Generating XML Data**: To generate XML data from a Python object, use the `ElementTree` class. The `Element()` function creates XML elements, and the `SubElement()` function adds child elements.

python

```python
import xml.etree.ElementTree as ET

# Create the root element
person = ET.Element('person')

# Add child elements
name = ET.SubElement(person, 'name')
name.text = 'Bob'
age = ET.SubElement(person, 'age')
age.text = '25'
city = ET.SubElement(person, 'city')
city.text = 'Los Angeles'

# Convert the ElementTree object to a
string
tree = ET.ElementTree(person)
tree.write('person.xml')  # Write to a file
```

  o **Explanation**:

- ET.Element() creates a new XML element, and ET.SubElement() creates a child element.
- The tree.write() method writes the XML data to a file.

- **Accessing XML Attributes**: XML elements can also have attributes. You can access them using the .attrib dictionary.

```python
xml_data = '''<person id="123">
            <name>Alice</name>
            <age>30</age>
            <city>New York</city>
        </person>'''

root = ET.fromstring(xml_data)
print(root.attrib['id'])  # Output: 123
```

   o **Explanation**:
      - root.attrib returns a dictionary of attributes for the element.

3. Project: Build a JSON-to-XML Converter

Now, let's build a simple project that converts JSON data into XML format. This will demonstrate how to work with both JSON and XML in Python.

- **Step 1: Define the JSON Data**: For this project, we will use a sample JSON object containing personal information.

```python
python

import json
import xml.etree.ElementTree as ET

# Sample JSON data
json_data = '''
{
    "person": {
        "name": "Alice",
        "age": 30,
        "city": "New York"
    }
}
'''

# Parse the JSON data
data = json.loads(json_data)
```

- **Step 2: Convert JSON to XML**: We'll create a function that converts the parsed JSON data into an XML format.

python

```python
def                       json_to_xml(json_obj,
root_element='root'):
    # Create the root element
    root = ET.Element(root_element)

    # Recursively convert JSON to XML
    def build_xml_element(obj, parent):
        if isinstance(obj, dict):
            for key, value in obj.items():
                element                     =
ET.SubElement(parent, key)
                build_xml_element(value,
element)
        elif isinstance(obj, list):
            for item in obj:
                item_element            =
ET.SubElement(parent, 'item')
                build_xml_element(item,
item_element)
        else:
            parent.text = str(obj)

    build_xml_element(json_obj, root)
    return ET.ElementTree(root)
```

168

```
# Convert the JSON data to XML
xml_tree = json_to_xml(data)


# Write the XML data to a file
xml_tree.write("output.xml")
```

- o **Explanation**:
  - The `json_to_xml` function converts a JSON object into an XML format by recursively creating XML elements for dictionaries and lists.
  - `build_xml_element` recursively iterates through the JSON object, creating elements for each key and adding them to the parent element.
  - The `xml_tree.write()` method writes the resulting XML structure to a file.
- **Step 3: Verify the Output**: After running the script, the XML file (`output.xml`) will be generated with the following content:

```
xml
```

```
<root>
    <person>
        <name>Alice</name>
        <age>30</age>
```

169

```
        <city>New York</city>
    </person>
</root>
```

Conclusion:

In this chapter, we learned how to handle both JSON and XML data in Python. We explored how to parse and generate JSON data using Python's `json` module and how to work with XML using the `xml.etree.ElementTree` module. You also applied these concepts by building a JSON-to-XML converter, demonstrating how to convert between these two popular data formats. With these skills, you can now easily handle and convert structured data in Python, making it easier to integrate with external APIs or process data from different sources.

CHAPTER 15

AUTOMATING TASKS WITH PYTHON

Overview:

One of Python's most powerful features is its ability to automate repetitive tasks. Whether you're managing files, sending emails, or generating reports, Python can help you save time and effort by automating these processes. In this chapter, we'll explore how to use Python to automate a variety of tasks. We will dive into automating file management, working with the `os` and `shutil` libraries, and automating emails. By the end of this chapter, you will build an automated report generator, which will demonstrate how to use Python to automate a real-world business task.

Topics Covered:

1. Automating File Management Tasks

Python makes it easy to automate common file management tasks such as moving, renaming, deleting, and organizing files. The `os` and `shutil` libraries provide a rich set of functions to interact with the file system.

171

- **Using the os Library for File Management**: The os library allows you to interact with the operating system and perform tasks like file manipulation, directory traversal, and more.

  o **Creating and Deleting Directories**:

  python

  ```python
  import os

  # Create a new directory
  os.mkdir('new_folder')

  # Delete an empty directory
  os.rmdir('new_folder')
  ```

  o **Renaming Files**:

  python

  ```python
  os.rename('old_name.txt',
  'new_name.txt')
  ```

  o **Listing Files in a Directory**:

  python

  ```python
  files                              =
  os.listdir('path/to/directory')
  for file in files:
  ```

172

```python
print(file)
```

- **Using the `shutil` Library for File Operations**: The `shutil` library provides higher-level file operations such as ing, moving, and removing files and directories.

  o **ing Files**:

  ```python
  python

  import shutil

  shutil.('source_file.txt',
  'destination_file.txt')
  ```

  o **Moving Files**:

  ```python
  python

  shutil.move('source_file.txt',
  'destination_folder')
  ```

  o **Deleting Files**:

  ```python
  python

  os.remove('file_to_delete.txt')
  ```

- **Automating File Organization**: You can write Python scripts to organize files based on their extensions, date modified, or other criteria. For example, you can automate the process of moving image files into an "Images" folder and document files into a "Documents" folder.

```python
import os
import shutil

def organize_files(directory):
    for filename in os.listdir(directory):
        file_path = os.path.join(directory, filename)
        if os.path.isfile(file_path):
            ext = os.path.splitext(filename)[1].lower()
            if ext in ['.jpg', '.jpeg', '.png']:
                target_folder = 'Images'
            elif ext in ['.pdf', '.txt', '.docx']:
                target_folder = 'Documents'
            else:
                target_folder = 'Others'

            target_folder_path = os.path.join(directory, target_folder)
            if not os.path.exists(target_folder_path):
```

174

```
os.makedirs(target_folder_path)

        shutil.move(file_path,
os.path.join(target_folder_path,
filename))
        print(f"Moved: {filename} to
{target_folder}/")
```

---

2. Working with the os and shutil Libraries

- **Managing File Paths**: Both os and shutil work with file paths to locate and manipulate files. You can use os.path to join paths, get absolute paths, and check for file existence.

  o **Joining File Paths**:

  python

  ```
  file_path = os.path.join('folder',
  'subfolder', 'file.txt')
  print(file_path)        # Output:
  folder/subfolder/file.txt
  ```

  o **Checking File Existence**:

  python

  ```
  if os.path.exists('file.txt'):
  ```

```
    print("File exists!")
else:
    print("File does not exist!")
```

- o **Getting Absolute Paths**:

  ```python
  ```

  ```python
  absolute_path                    =
  os.path.abspath('file.txt')
  print(absolute_path)
  ```

- o **Removing Directories**: If the directory is not empty, you can remove it using `shutil.rmtree()`:

  ```python
  ```

  ```python
  shutil.rmtree('folder_to_delete')    #
  Deletes folder and its contents
  ```

---

3. Automating Emails with Python

Sending automated emails can be useful for tasks such as sending reports, reminders, or notifications. Python provides the `smtplib` library to send emails through an SMTP server.

- **Setting Up SMTP for Sending Emails**: First, you need to configure the SMTP server. For example, if you're using Gmail, you would set up the Gmail SMTP server.

python

```python
import smtplib
from       email.mime.multipart       import
MIMEMultipart
from email.mime.text import MIMEText

def send_email(subject, body, to_email):
    # Email credentials
    from_email = 'your_email@gmail.com'
    password = 'your_email_password'

    # Set up the MIME
    msg = MIMEMultipart()
    msg['From'] = from_email
    msg['To'] = to_email
    msg['Subject'] = subject

    # Attach the body with the msg instance
    msg.attach(MIMEText(body, 'plain'))

    # Set up the server
    server                                    =
smtplib.SMTP('smtp.gmail.com', 587)
    server.starttls()  # Enable security
```

```
# Log in to the email server
server.login(from_email, password)

# Send the email
text = msg.as_string()
server.sendmail(from_email, to_email,
text)

# Quit the server
server.quit()

print("Email sent successfully!")
```

- o **Explanation**:
    - `smtplib.SMTP('smtp.gmail.com', 587)` sets up the Gmail SMTP server.
    - `msg.attach(MIMEText(body, 'plain'))` attaches the body of the email.
    - `server.login()` authenticates the email account.
- **Sending HTML Emails**: You can send HTML emails by changing the MIME type.

```python
python
```

```
msg.attach(MIMEText('<h1>HTML
Email</h1><p>This is an HTML email.</p>',
'html'))
```

- **Handling Email Attachments**: You can attach files to emails using the `MIMEBase` class.

python

```
from email.mime.base import MIMEBase
from email import encoders

filename = 'report.pdf'
attachment = open(filename, 'rb')

part = MIMEBase('application', 'octet-
stream')
part.set_payload(attachment.read())
encoders.encode_base64(part)

part.add_header('Content-Disposition',
f'attachment; filename={filename}')
msg.attach(part)
```

4. Project: Build an Automated Report Generator

In this project, you'll build a script that generates a report and sends it automatically via email. The report will be based on data from a file, such as a CSV file containing sales data.

- **Step 1: Generate a Report**: For the report, you can process data from a CSV file or other data sources and generate a summary. For example, you can calculate the total sales for each product and generate a simple report.

python

```python
import csv

def generate_report(filename):
    with open(filename, 'r') as file:
        reader = csv.reader(file)
        next(reader)  # Skip the header row

        total_sales = 0
        for row in reader:
            total_sales += float(row[2])
# Assuming the third column is sales data

        return        f"Total        sales:
${total_sales:.2f}"

report = generate_report('sales_data.csv')
```

- **Step 2: Send the Report via Email**: Once the report is generated, you can send it via email using the send_email function we defined earlier.

python

```
subject = "Monthly Sales Report"
body = f"Hello,\n\nPlease find the monthly
sales   report   below:\n\n{report}\n\nBest
regards."
to_email = 'recipient@example.com'

send_email(subject, body, to_email)
```

- **Step 3: Automate the Report Generation and Sending**: You can schedule this script to run automatically at regular intervals (e.g., once a month) using task schedulers such as `cron` on Linux or Task Scheduler on Windows.

Conclusion:

In this chapter, you learned how to automate a variety of tasks with Python, including file management, sending emails, and generating reports. You explored how to use the `os` and `shutil` libraries for file manipulation, how to automate email sending using `smtplib`, and how to create an automated report generator. Automation with Python can significantly improve your productivity by handling repetitive tasks, and with these skills, you can build more advanced automation solutions for your personal or business needs.

CHAPTER 16

TESTING AND DEBUGGING PYTHON CODE

Overview:

Testing and debugging are essential skills for every programmer. Writing tests ensures that your code works as expected, while debugging helps you identify and fix issues in your code. In this chapter, we will explore best practices for testing and debugging Python code. You will learn how to use popular testing frameworks like `unittest` and `pytest`, write effective unit tests, and employ debugging techniques with Python's built-in tools like `pdb` and `logging`. Finally, you will apply these skills to build a Python application with test cases.

Topics Covered:

1. Using `unittest` and `pytest` for Testing

Testing frameworks like `unittest` and `pytest` make it easy to write and organize tests for your Python code. They provide powerful tools to help you automate the testing process and ensure the correctness of your code.

- **Using unittest for Testing**: unittest is a built-in Python module that provides a framework for writing and running tests. It is based on the xUnit testing framework and supports test organization, setup, and teardown.

  - **Creating a Simple Test Case**: To create a test case, you subclass the unittest.TestCase class and define test methods using the test_ prefix.

    python

    ```python
    import unittest

    # Function to be tested
    def add(a, b):
        return a + b

    class TestMathOperations(unittest.TestCas
    e):
        def test_add(self):
            self.assertEqual(add(2,   3),
    5)   # Test if 2 + 3 equals 5

    if __name__ == "__main__":
        unittest.main()
    ```

  - **Explanation**:

- - unittest.main() runs all test methods defined in the TestMathOperations class.
  - self.assertEqual() checks if the result of add(2, 3) is equal to 5.
  - o **Running Tests**: To run the tests, simply execute the script:

```bash
```

```
python test_math_operations.py
```

- **Using pytest for Testing**: pytest is a third-party testing framework that makes it easier to write and run tests. It is more flexible and feature-rich than unittest.
  - o **Installing pytest**: To install pytest, run:

```bash
```

```
pip install pytest
```

  - o **Writing Tests with pytest**: pytest does not require you to subclass TestCase. You just write functions that start with test_ and use assertions.

```python
```

```
# Function to be tested
def subtract(a, b):
    return a - b

# Test function
def test_subtract():
    assert subtract(5, 3) == 2    #
Test if 5 - 3 equals 2
```

- o **Running Tests with `pytest`**: To run the tests, simply execute the following command in the terminal:

```bash
pytest test_math_operations.py
```

- o **Test Output**: `pytest` provides a detailed output, including which tests passed, which failed, and why.

---

2. Writing Effective Unit Tests

Unit tests focus on testing individual units of functionality in isolation. Here are some best practices for writing effective unit tests:

- **Write Small, Focused Tests**: Each test should focus on a single behavior. If a test is doing too much, it's harder to understand and maintain.
- **Use Assertions**: Assertions are the core of any test. Common assertions include:
  - `assertEqual(a, b)`: Tests if a equals b.
  - `assertTrue(x)`: Tests if x is true.
  - `assertFalse(x)`: Tests if x is false.
  - `assertRaises(exception)`: Tests if a specific exception is raised.

python

```python
def divide(a, b):
    if b == 0:
        raise ValueError("Cannot divide by zero")
    return a / b

def test_divide():
    assert divide(6, 3) == 2
    with pytest.raises(ValueError):
        divide(6, 0)
```

- **Test for Edge Cases**: Ensure that you test for edge cases such as empty inputs, very large numbers, or invalid data. These tests help ensure that your code is robust and can handle unexpected situations.

186

- **Use Mocking**: Sometimes, you need to test functions that interact with external systems (e.g., a database, API, or filesystem). In these cases, you can use mocking to simulate these interactions and focus on testing the function's behavior.

```python
from unittest.mock import MagicMock

# Mocking a function that interacts with an
external API
api_call                                =
MagicMock(return_value={'status':
'success'})
assert api_call() == {'status': 'success'}
```

3. Debugging Techniques with `pdb` *and* `logging`

Debugging is a critical part of the development process. Python provides powerful tools for debugging and logging, which help you identify and fix issues in your code.

- **Using pdb for Interactive Debugging**: The pdb (Python Debugger) module allows you to set breakpoints in your code and interactively inspect the program's state during execution.

○ **Setting a Breakpoint**: You can set a breakpoint by inserting `pdb.set_trace()` in your code at the point where you want to start debugging.

```python
import pdb

def multiply(a, b):
    result = a * b
    pdb.set_trace()    # Start the debugger here
    return result

multiply(3, 4)
```

○ **Debugging Commands**: Once the debugger is triggered, you can use commands like:
  - n: Step to the next line.
  - c: Continue execution.
  - q: Quit the debugger.

- **Using `logging` for Debugging and Monitoring**: The `logging` module allows you to log messages at various severity levels (DEBUG, INFO, WARNING, ERROR, CRITICAL).

```python
```

```
import logging

logging.basicConfig(level=logging.DEBUG)
# Set logging level to DEBUG

logging.debug("This is a debug message")
logging.info("This is an info message")
logging.warning("This    is    a    warning
message")
logging.error("This is an error message")
logging.critical("This    is    a    critical
message")
```

- o **Explanation**:
  - The `logging.basicConfig()` function sets up the logging configuration.
  - Use `logging.debug()` for low-level information, and `logging.error()` for error messages.
  - Logs can be written to the console or saved to a file for later analysis.

---

4. Project: Build a Python Application with Test Cases

Now, let's apply what we've learned and build a Python application that includes both functional code and test cases. In this project, we'll create a simple "Shopping Cart" class and write unit tests for it.

- **Step 1: Create the `ShoppingCart` Class**:

python

```python
class ShoppingCart:
    def __init__(self):
        self.items = {}

    def add_item(self, item, price, quantity=1):
        if item in self.items:
            self.items[item]['quantity'] += quantity
        else:
            self.items[item] = {'price': price, 'quantity': quantity}

    def total_cost(self):
        return sum(item['price'] * item['quantity'] for item in self.items.values())

    def remove_item(self, item):
        if item in self.items:
            del self.items[item]
```

- **Step 2: Write Unit Tests for `ShoppingCart`**:

```python
python

import unittest

class TestShoppingCart(unittest.TestCase):
    def test_add_item(self):
        cart = ShoppingCart()
        cart.add_item("apple", 1.5, 2)

self.assertEqual(cart.total_cost(), 3.0)

    def test_remove_item(self):
        cart = ShoppingCart()
        cart.add_item("banana", 1.2, 3)
        cart.remove_item("banana")

self.assertEqual(cart.total_cost(), 0)

    def test_multiple_items(self):
        cart = ShoppingCart()
        cart.add_item("apple", 1.5, 2)
        cart.add_item("banana", 1.2, 3)

self.assertEqual(cart.total_cost(), 5.1)
```

- **Step 3: Running the Tests**: To run the tests, simply execute:

```bash
bash
```

```
python -m unittest test_shopping_cart.py
```

This will run the test methods and provide feedback on which tests passed or failed.

Conclusion:

In this chapter, we learned how to effectively test and debug Python code. You were introduced to testing frameworks like unittest and pytest for writing unit tests, as well as best practices for writing effective tests. We also explored debugging techniques with Python's pdb debugger and the logging module. Finally, you applied these techniques by building a Python application—ShoppingCart—and writing test cases to validate its functionality. With these tools, you are now equipped to write reliable, maintainable Python code and efficiently debug and test your applications.

CHAPTER 17

INTRODUCTION TO MACHINE LEARNING WITH PYTHON

Overview:

Machine learning (ML) is a powerful field that enables computers to learn from data and make predictions or decisions without being explicitly programmed. In this chapter, we will introduce the core concepts of machine learning and how to implement them using Python. We will cover the basics of ML, how to use the popular `scikit-learn` library for machine learning tasks, and how to build a basic classifier model. Finally, you will apply your knowledge to build a sentiment analysis model, a classic natural language processing (NLP) task that classifies text as positive or negative.

Topics Covered:

1. Introduction to Machine Learning Concepts

Machine learning is the study of algorithms that can learn from and make predictions on data. The field can be broadly categorized into three types:

- **Supervised Learning**: In supervised learning, the model is trained on labeled data, meaning the input data is paired with the correct output. The model learns to predict the output for unseen data. Common tasks include classification (predicting categories) and regression (predicting continuous values).
    - Example: Predicting house prices based on features like size and location (regression).
    - Example: Classifying emails as spam or not spam (classification).
- **Unsupervised Learning**: Unsupervised learning involves training a model on data without labeled outputs. The model tries to find patterns or groupings in the data. Common tasks include clustering (grouping similar data points) and dimensionality reduction (simplifying data while preserving important information).
    - Example: Clustering customers into different segments based on their purchasing behavior.
- **Reinforcement Learning**: In reinforcement learning, an agent learns by interacting with an environment and receiving rewards or penalties based on its actions. It is commonly used in robotics, gaming, and autonomous systems.
    - Example: Training a robot to navigate a maze.

- **Evaluation Metrics**: Evaluation metrics are used to assess the performance of machine learning models. Common metrics for classification tasks include:

  o **Accuracy**: The proportion of correctly predicted instances.

  o **Precision and Recall**: Metrics used to assess the quality of the predictions, especially in imbalanced datasets.

  o **F1 Score**: The harmonic mean of precision and recall.

---

2. Using `scikit-learn` *for ML Tasks*

`scikit-learn` is one of the most widely used Python libraries for machine learning. It provides simple and efficient tools for data mining and data analysis. In this section, you'll learn how to use `scikit-learn` for basic machine learning tasks like loading datasets, splitting data, training models, and making predictions.

- **Installing `scikit-learn`**: First, you need to install the scikit-learn library:

```bash

pip install scikit-learn
```

- **Loading a Dataset**: `scikit-learn` provides built-in datasets that you can use for practice. The `load_iris()` function loads the Iris dataset, which is commonly used for classification tasks.

python

```
from sklearn.datasets import load_iris
iris = load_iris()
X = iris.data  # Features
y = iris.target  # Labels
```

- **Splitting Data into Training and Test Sets**: It's important to evaluate the model on unseen data, so you need to split your dataset into a training set and a test set. The `train_test_split()` function makes this easy.

python

```
from     sklearn.model_selection     import
train_test_split
X_train,   X_test,   y_train,   y_test   =
train_test_split(X,   y,   test_size=0.2,
random_state=42)
```

- **Training a Model**: Scikit-learn provides many built-in models for classification and regression. For this example, we'll use a simple classifier, such as the k-Nearest Neighbors (k-NN) algorithm.

```
python

from        sklearn.neighbors        import
KNeighborsClassifier

# Create the model
model                                =
KNeighborsClassifier(n_neighbors=3)

# Train the model
model.fit(X_train, y_train)
```

- **Making Predictions**: After training the model, you can use it to make predictions on the test set.

```
python

y_pred = model.predict(X_test)
```

- **Evaluating the Model**: You can evaluate the model's performance using metrics like accuracy:

```
python

from sklearn.metrics import accuracy_score
accuracy = accuracy_score(y_test, y_pred)
print(f"Accuracy: {accuracy * 100:.2f}%")
```

3. Building a Basic Classifier Model

In this section, we will walk through the steps of building a classifier model using the `scikit-learn` library. We will use the `Iris` dataset and train a simple classifier to predict the species of a flower based on its features (sepal length, sepal width, petal length, and petal width).

- **Step 1: Load the Dataset**:

  python

  ```
  from sklearn.datasets import load_iris
  iris = load_iris()
  X = iris.data   # Features
  y = iris.target   # Labels
  ```

- **Step 2: Split the Data**:

  python

  ```
  from     sklearn.model_selection     import
  train_test_split
  X_train,   X_test,   y_train,   y_test   =
  train_test_split(X,    y,    test_size=0.2,
  random_state=42)
  ```

- **Step 3: Train the Model**: We will use the `KNeighborsClassifier` for this task.

python

```
from        sklearn.neighbors        import
KNeighborsClassifier

model                                  =
KNeighborsClassifier(n_neighbors=3)
model.fit(X_train, y_train)
```

- **Step 4: Make Predictions**:

python

```
y_pred = model.predict(X_test)
```

- **Step 5: Evaluate the Model**:

python

```
from sklearn.metrics import accuracy_score
accuracy = accuracy_score(y_test, y_pred)
print(f"Accuracy: {accuracy * 100:.2f}%")
```

---

4. Project: Build a Sentiment Analysis Model

In this project, you will build a sentiment analysis model that classifies text data as either positive or negative. We'll use the scikit-learn library to create a machine learning model that can analyze and predict sentiment from text.

- **Step 1: Load the Dataset**: We'll use a sample dataset of movie reviews. The `load_files()` function from `scikit-learn` is used to load text files into a dataset.

python

```python
from sklearn.datasets import load_files

# Load the dataset of movie reviews
data = load_files('movie_reviews')
X = data.data  # Reviews (text)
y = data.target  # Sentiments (positive/negative)
```

- **Step 2: Preprocess the Text Data**: Before training the model, we need to convert the text data into a numerical format. We'll use `TfidfVectorizer` to convert the text into TF-IDF features.

python

```python
from sklearn.feature_extraction.text import TfidfVectorizer

vectorizer = TfidfVectorizer(stop_words='english')
X_tfidf = vectorizer.fit_transform(X)
```

- **Step 3: Split the Data**:

python

```
from     sklearn.model_selection    import
train_test_split
X_train,   X_test,   y_train,   y_test   =
train_test_split(X_tfidf,              y,
test_size=0.2, random_state=42)
```

- **Step 4: Train a Classifier**: For sentiment analysis, we can use a `MultinomialNB` (Naive Bayes) classifier.

python

```
from        sklearn.naive_bayes       import
MultinomialNB

model = MultinomialNB()
model.fit(X_train, y_train)
```

- **Step 5: Evaluate the Model**: After training the model, we can evaluate its performance using accuracy and confusion matrix.

python

```
from          sklearn.metrics         import
accuracy_score, confusion_matrix

y_pred = model.predict(X_test)
accuracy = accuracy_score(y_test, y_pred)
```

201

```
print(f"Accuracy: {accuracy * 100:.2f}%")
print(f"Confusion
Matrix:\n{confusion_matrix(y_test,
y_pred)}")
```

Conclusion:

In this chapter, we introduced you to the fundamentals of machine learning using Python. You learned about the core concepts of machine learning, including supervised learning, and how to use the `scikit-learn` library for tasks such as classification. We also walked through the process of building a basic classifier model and a sentiment analysis project. Machine learning opens up many possibilities for working with data and automating decision-making processes, and with Python, you have a powerful set of tools to get started with ML tasks.

CHAPTER 18

INTRODUCTION TO DEEP LEARNING WITH PYTHON

Overview:

Deep learning is a subset of machine learning that uses neural networks to model and solve complex tasks such as image classification, natural language processing, and game playing. In this chapter, we will introduce the core concepts of deep learning, including neural networks and their architecture. We will use TensorFlow and Keras, popular frameworks for building and training deep learning models in Python. By the end of this chapter, you will have built a simple neural network model and applied it to a real-world project: digit recognition using the MNIST dataset.

Topics Covered:

1. Basics of Neural Networks

Neural networks are computational models inspired by the human brain. They consist of layers of neurons (nodes) that work together to learn patterns from data. Each neuron receives input, processes it, and produces an output that is passed to the next layer of neurons.

- **Structure of a Neural Network**: A neural network typically consists of three types of layers:
  - **Input Layer**: The first layer that receives the data (features).
  - **Hidden Layers**: Intermediate layers that process the inputs and learn features.
  - **Output Layer**: The final layer that produces the predictions or classifications.
- **Neurons and Activation Functions**: Each neuron processes the input it receives, applies a weight, adds a bias, and passes the result through an activation function. The activation function determines the neuron's output.
  - **Common Activation Functions**:
    - **ReLU (Rectified Linear Unit)**: `f(x) = max(0, x)` (commonly used in hidden layers).
    - **Sigmoid**: `f(x) = 1 / (1 + exp(-x))` (often used for binary classification).
    - **Softmax**: Used for multi-class classification (outputs probabilities for each class).
- **Training a Neural Network**: The training process involves using a dataset to adjust the weights and biases

of the network to minimize the error between the predicted and actual outputs. This is done using optimization algorithms such as **Gradient Descent** and backpropagation.

2. Introduction to TensorFlow and Keras

TensorFlow is an open-source framework for building and deploying machine learning models. **Keras** is an easy-to-use high-level API that runs on top of TensorFlow, making it simple to define and train deep learning models.

- **Installing TensorFlow**: To install TensorFlow and Keras, run the following command:

```bash

pip install tensorflow
```

- **Getting Started with TensorFlow and Keras**: TensorFlow and Keras provide built-in functions to create, compile, and train models.
  - o **Creating a Sequential Model**: In Keras, the `Sequential` model is a linear stack of layers. You can define the model by adding layers one by one.

```python
python


from tensorflow.keras.models import
Sequential
from tensorflow.keras.layers import
Dense

model = Sequential([
    Dense(128,    activation='relu',
input_shape=(784,)),    # Hidden layer
with 128 neurons
    Dense(10,    activation='softmax')
# Output layer with 10 neurons (for
10 classes)
])
```

o **Compiling the Model**: After defining the model, you compile it by specifying the optimizer, loss function, and evaluation metric.

```python
python


model.compile(optimizer='adam',
loss='sparse_categorical_crossentro
py', metrics=['accuracy'])
```

o **Training the Model**: You can train the model using the fit() method, which takes the training data, labels, and the number of epochs to train.

```python
model.fit(X_train,        y_train,
epochs=5)
```

---

3. Building a Simple Neural Network

Now that we have covered the basics of neural networks and how to use TensorFlow and Keras, let's build a simple neural network model that can classify handwritten digits using the MNIST dataset.

- **Step 1: Load the MNIST Dataset**: MNIST is a dataset of 28x28 grayscale images of handwritten digits (0–9). It is commonly used for training machine learning models.

```python
from    tensorflow.keras.datasets    import
mnist

# Load the MNIST dataset
(X_train,  y_train),  (X_test,  y_test)  =
mnist.load_data()

# Normalize the images to values between 0
and 1
```

207

```
X_train, X_test = X_train / 255.0, X_test
/ 255.0
```

- o **Explanation**:
    - `mnist.load_data()` loads the MNIST training and test datasets.
    - The pixel values of the images are scaled to the range [0, 1] for better training performance.
- **Step 2: Define the Neural Network Model**: We'll create a simple neural network with one hidden layer of 128 neurons and an output layer with 10 neurons (one for each digit).

python

```
model = Sequential([
    Dense(128,          activation='relu',
input_shape=(784,)),    # Flattened 28x28
image
    Dense(10, activation='softmax')   # 10
output neurons for 10 classes (digits 0-9)
])
```

- o **Flatten Layer**: Since the MNIST images are 28x28 arrays, we need to flatten them into 1D vectors (784 elements). This can be done with

Flatten() (or by specifying input_shape in the first Dense layer).

```python
model.add(Flatten(input_shape=(28, 28)))
```

- **Step 3: Compile and Train the Model**: We compile the model with the adam optimizer and sparse_categorical_crossentropy loss function (since this is a multi-class classification problem).

```python
model.compile(optimizer='adam',
loss='sparse_categorical_crossentropy',
metrics=['accuracy'])
model.fit(X_train, y_train, epochs=5)
```

- **Step 4: Evaluate the Model**: After training the model, evaluate its performance on the test dataset.

```python
test_loss,          test_acc          =
model.evaluate(X_test, y_test, verbose=2)
print(f"Test accuracy: {test_acc}")
```

4. Project: Build a Digit Recognition Model Using MNIST

In this project, we will build and train a digit recognition model that classifies handwritten digits using the MNIST dataset.

- **Step 1: Import Required Libraries**:

  python

  ```python
  import tensorflow as tf
  from      tensorflow.keras.models      import
  Sequential
  from tensorflow.keras.layers import Dense,
  Flatten
  ```

- **Step 2: Load and Preprocess the Dataset**:

  python

  ```python
  # Load MNIST dataset
  (X_train,  y_train),  (X_test,  y_test)  =
  tf.keras.datasets.mnist.load_data()

  # Normalize the images
  X_train, X_test = X_train / 255.0, X_test
  / 255.0

  # Flatten the images to 1D vectors (28x28
  -> 784)
  X_train = X_train.reshape(-1, 28 * 28)
  ```

210

```
X_test = X_test.reshape(-1, 28 * 28)
```

- **Step 3: Define the Neural Network Model**:

python

```
model = Sequential([
    Flatten(input_shape=(784,)),          #
Flatten 28x28 image into a vector
    Dense(128, activation='relu'),
    Dense(10, activation='softmax')   # 10
output classes for digits 0-9
])
```

- **Step 4: Compile the Model**:

python

```
model.compile(optimizer='adam',
loss='sparse_categorical_crossentropy',
metrics=['accuracy'])
```

- **Step 5: Train the Model**:

python

```
model.fit(X_train, y_train, epochs=5)
```

- **Step 6: Evaluate the Model**:

```
python
```

```
test_loss,            test_acc         =
model.evaluate(X_test, y_test)
print(f"Test accuracy: {test_acc}")
```

- **Step 7: Making Predictions**: You can use the trained model to make predictions on new images.

```
python
```

```
predictions = model.predict(X_test[:5])   #
Predict the first 5 test images
print(predictions)   # Output: Probability
scores for each class
```

Conclusion:

In this chapter, we introduced deep learning concepts and how to build and train deep learning models in Python using TensorFlow and Keras. You learned the basics of neural networks, including layers, neurons, activation functions, and training processes. We used `scikit-learn` for building a simple neural network, and then transitioned to TensorFlow to build a digit recognition model using the MNIST dataset. Deep learning opens up exciting opportunities for solving complex problems such as image classification, speech recognition, and more, and with TensorFlow and Keras, you have the tools to start exploring these possibilities.

CHAPTER 19

DATA VISUALIZATION WITH MATPLOTLIB AND SEABORN

Overview:

Data visualization is a powerful tool for understanding, interpreting, and presenting data. Python offers excellent libraries for creating visualizations, with **Matplotlib** and **Seaborn** being two of the most popular. In this chapter, we will explore how to create basic and advanced plots using these libraries. We will cover plotting techniques that help reveal trends, relationships, and patterns in data. By the end of this chapter, you will be able to visualize data effectively and create interactive charts for data exploration.

Topics Covered:

1. Creating Basic Plots with Matplotlib

Matplotlib is the foundational Python plotting library. It offers flexibility to create a wide range of static, animated, and interactive plots.

- **Installing Matplotlib**: If you don't have Matplotlib installed, you can install it using pip:

```bash
pip install matplotlib
```

- **Creating a Simple Line Plot**: The most basic plot in Matplotlib is the line plot, which is often used to visualize continuous data over a range (such as time series data).

```python
import matplotlib.pyplot as plt

# Sample data
x = [0, 1, 2, 3, 4]
y = [0, 1, 4, 9, 16]

# Create a basic line plot
plt.plot(x, y)
plt.title("Simple Line Plot")
plt.xlabel("X-axis")
plt.ylabel("Y-axis")
plt.show()  # Display the plot
```

  o **Explanation**:

    ▪ `plt.plot(x, y)` creates the line plot.

- plt.title(), plt.xlabel(), and plt.ylabel() are used to add a title and labels to the axes.
- plt.show() displays the plot in a window.

- **Creating a Scatter Plot**: A scatter plot is useful for visualizing the relationship between two variables.

```python
x = [1, 2, 3, 4, 5]
y = [5, 4, 3, 2, 1]

plt.scatter(x, y)
plt.title("Scatter Plot")
plt.xlabel("X-axis")
plt.ylabel("Y-axis")
plt.show()
```

- **Creating a Bar Chart**: A bar chart is used for comparing quantities across different categories.

```python
categories = ['A', 'B', 'C', 'D']
values = [5, 3, 9, 6]

plt.bar(categories, values)
plt.title("Bar Chart")
```

```
plt.xlabel("Categories")
plt.ylabel("Values")
plt.show()
```

2. Advanced Visualizations with Seaborn

Seaborn is built on top of Matplotlib and provides a high-level interface for creating more advanced statistical plots. It is particularly useful for visualizing the relationship between variables and creating more informative charts with less code.

- **Installing Seaborn**: If you don't have Seaborn installed, you can install it using pip:

```bash
pip install seaborn
```

- **Creating a Distribution Plot**: Seaborn's `distplot()` function allows you to visualize the distribution of a dataset. This is useful for understanding the shape and spread of the data.

```python
import seaborn as sns
import numpy as np
```

216

```
# Generate random data
data = np.random.normal(size=1000)


sns.distplot(data, kde=True, bins=30)
plt.title("Distribution Plot")
plt.show()
```

- o **Explanation**:
  - `distplot()` creates a histogram of the data and includes a Kernel Density Estimate (KDE) curve.
  - `bins=30` specifies the number of bins for the histogram.
  - `kde=True` adds the smooth KDE curve.
- **Creating a Box Plot**: A box plot is useful for visualizing the spread and distribution of data, as well as detecting outliers.

```python

data = np.random.normal(size=100)


sns.boxplot(data=data)
plt.title("Box Plot")
plt.show()
```

- **Heatmaps**: Seaborn's `heatmap()` function can visualize matrix-like data, such as correlation matrices or confusion matrices.

python

```
# Create a correlation matrix
data = np.random.rand(10, 12)
correlation_matrix = np.corrcoef(data)

sns.heatmap(correlation_matrix,
annot=True, cmap='coolwarm')
plt.title("Heatmap")
plt.show()
```

  o **Explanation**:
    - `np.corrcoef(data)` calculates the correlation matrix for the dataset.
    - `sns.heatmap()` visualizes the matrix, with `annot=True` showing the values in each cell.

- **Pair Plot**: A pair plot creates a grid of scatter plots for visualizing relationships between all pairs of features in a dataset.

python

```
# Load the iris dataset
```

```
from sklearn.datasets import load_iris
iris = load_iris()

sns.pairplot(iris.data,
hue=iris.target_names[iris.target])
plt.title("Pair Plot")
plt.show()
```

- o **Explanation**:
  - `pairplot()` plots pairwise relationships in a dataset, colored by the class labels (in this case, `iris.target_names`).

---

3. Plotting Statistical Data

Data visualization is often used to reveal statistical insights from a dataset. Here are some ways to visualize statistical data using Matplotlib and Seaborn.

- **Creating a Regression Plot**: Regression plots help visualize the relationship between two variables and can be used to fit a regression line.

```python
sns.regplot(x="sepal length (cm)",
y="sepal width (cm)", data=iris)
```

```
plt.title("Regression Plot")
plt.show()
```

- **Plotting Correlation**: Visualizing the correlation matrix of a dataset helps identify relationships between different features.

python

```
correlation_matrix = iris.data.corr()
sns.heatmap(correlation_matrix,
annot=True, cmap="coolwarm")
plt.title("Correlation Heatmap")
plt.show()
```

4. Project: Visualize a Dataset Using Interactive Charts

In this project, we will visualize a real-world dataset using interactive charts to gain insights. We'll use the **Iris dataset** to create several interactive visualizations, including a scatter plot, pair plot, and heatmap.

- **Step 1: Load the Dataset**: The Iris dataset contains information about iris flowers, including features like sepal length, sepal width, petal length, and petal width. We will load the dataset from `sklearn.datasets`.

python

```
from sklearn.datasets import load_iris
import seaborn as sns
import matplotlib.pyplot as plt

iris = load_iris()
iris_data = iris.data
iris_target = iris.target
iris_feature_names = iris.feature_names
iris_target_names = iris.target_names
```

- **Step 2: Create an Interactive Scatter Plot**: We will create an interactive scatter plot to visualize the relationship between two features, such as sepal length and sepal width.

python

```
sns.scatterplot(x=iris_data[:,          0],
y=iris_data[:,                          1],
hue=iris_target_names[iris_target],
palette="Set1")
plt.title("Sepal Length vs Sepal Width")
plt.xlabel("Sepal Length")
plt.ylabel("Sepal Width")
plt.show()
```

- **Step 3: Create an Interactive Pair Plot**: A pair plot shows pairwise relationships between all features in the dataset.

python

```
import pandas as pd
iris_df      =      pd.DataFrame(iris_data,
columns=iris_feature_names)
iris_df['species']                        =
iris_target_names[iris_target]

sns.pairplot(iris_df,        hue="species",
palette="Set2")
plt.title("Pair Plot of Iris Dataset")
plt.show()
```

- **Step 4: Create an Interactive Heatmap**: A heatmap can help visualize correlations between features in the dataset.

python

```
correlation_matrix = iris_df.corr()
sns.heatmap(correlation_matrix,
annot=True,              cmap="coolwarm",
linewidths=0.5)
plt.title("Correlation Heatmap")
plt.show()
```

Conclusion:

In this chapter, we learned how to create a variety of visualizations in Python using Matplotlib and Seaborn. You explored basic plots like line plots, scatter plots, and bar charts, as well as advanced visualizations such as heatmaps, pair plots, and regression plots. By visualizing statistical data, you can gain insights into the structure and relationships within your data. You also applied these skills by building an interactive project that visualized the Iris dataset using different types of plots. Data visualization is a crucial part of the data analysis process, and with these tools, you can effectively communicate patterns and trends in your data.

CHAPTER 20

BUILDING RESTFUL APIS WITH FLASK

Overview:

In this chapter, you will learn how to build RESTful APIs using **Flask**, a lightweight web framework for Python. REST (Representational State Transfer) is a popular architectural style for building APIs, which allows different applications to communicate with each other over HTTP. Flask provides an easy and efficient way to build RESTful APIs, making it a great choice for Python developers. We will cover how to handle HTTP methods like GET, POST, PUT, and DELETE, as well as how to authenticate users using JSON Web Tokens (JWT). By the end of this chapter, you will have built a simple task management API.

Topics Covered:

1. Creating RESTful APIs with Flask

Flask is a lightweight and flexible web framework for building APIs. It is particularly useful for creating RESTful services due to its simplicity and ease of use. To get started, you need to install Flask and Flask-RESTful.

- **Installing Flask and Flask-RESTful**: First, install Flask and Flask-RESTful using pip:

```bash
pip install Flask Flask-RESTful
```

- **Setting Up a Basic Flask Application**: Here's how you can create a basic Flask app that serves a simple endpoint.

```python
from flask import Flask
from flask_restful import Api, Resource

# Initialize Flask app and API
app = Flask(__name__)
api = Api(app)

# Define a simple resource
class HelloWorld(Resource):
    def get(self):
        return {'message': 'Hello,
World!'}

# Add resource to API
```

225

```
api.add_resource(HelloWorld, '/')

if __name__ == '__main__':
    app.run(debug=True)
```

- o **Explanation**:
  - `Flask(__name__)`: Initializes the Flask application.
  - `Api(app)`: Initializes Flask-RESTful's API.
  - `class HelloWorld(Resource)`: Defines a RESTful resource with a `get()` method to handle GET requests.
  - `api.add_resource(HelloWorld, '/')`: Adds the `HelloWorld` resource to the API, accessible at the root URL (`/`).
- o **Running the Application**: To run the application, save the code to a file (e.g., `app.py`) and execute it:

```bash
```

```
python app.py
```

Navigate to `http://127.0.0.1:5000/` in your browser, and you should see the response `{"message": "Hello, World!"}`.

226

2. Handling HTTP Methods (GET, POST, PUT, DELETE)

RESTful APIs typically expose several endpoints that correspond to different HTTP methods: GET, POST, PUT, and DELETE. These methods allow clients to interact with the server in various ways.

- **GET Method**: The GET method is used to retrieve data from the server.

```python
class Task(Resource):
    def get(self, task_id):
        return    {'task_id':    task_id,
'status': 'pending'}

api.add_resource(Task,
'/task/<int:task_id>')
```

- o **Explanation**:
  - The get() method retrieves information about a specific task based on its task_id.
  - task_id is passed as a URL parameter (/task/<int:task_id>).

- **POST Method**: The POST method is used to create new resources.

```python
from flask import request

class TaskList(Resource):
    def post(self):
        data = request.get_json()   # Get JSON data from request
        task_name = data.get('task_name')
        return {'task_name': task_name, 'status': 'created'}, 201

api.add_resource(TaskList, '/tasks')
```

- **Explanation**:
  - The post() method receives data in the request body (in JSON format).
  - request.get_json() is used to parse the JSON data and extract the task name.

- **PUT Method**: The PUT method is used to update an existing resource.

```python
class Task(Resource):
    def put(self, task_id):
```

```
data = request.get_json()
task_name = data.get('task_name')
return    {'task_id':    task_id,
'task_name':    task_name,    'status':
'updated'}


api.add_resource(Task,
'/task/<int:task_id>')
```

    o **Explanation**:

        ■ The `put()` method updates an existing task, identified by `task_id`, with new data provided in the request body.

- **DELETE Method**: The DELETE method is used to delete an existing resource.

```
python


class Task(Resource):
    def delete(self, task_id):
        return    {'message':    f'Task
{task_id} deleted'}


api.add_resource(Task,
'/task/<int:task_id>')
```

    o **Explanation**:

        ■ The `delete()` method deletes a task with the specified `task_id`.

229

3. Authenticating Users with JWT Tokens

Authentication is crucial in many applications. One common method of authentication in RESTful APIs is using **JSON Web Tokens (JWT)**. JWTs allow clients to authenticate with the server by sending a token with each request.

- **Installing PyJWT**: To work with JWTs, we need the `pyjwt` library. Install it using pip:

  bash

  ```
  pip install pyjwt
  ```

- **Creating JWT Tokens**: The server will issue a JWT token when the user logs in. You can generate a token using the `pyjwt` library.

  python

  ```
  import jwt
  from datetime import datetime, timedelta

  SECRET_KEY = 'your_secret_key'

  def generate_token(user_id):
      expiration = datetime.utcnow() +
  timedelta(hours=1)
  ```

```
    payload = {'user_id': user_id, 'exp':
expiration}
    token        =        jwt.encode(payload,
SECRET_KEY, algorithm='HS256')
    return token
```

- o **Explanation**:
  - ▪ `jwt.encode()` generates the token using a payload that includes the `user_id` and an expiration time.
  - ▪ The `SECRET_KEY` is used to sign the token to ensure its authenticity.

- **Verifying JWT Tokens**: The server verifies the JWT token sent by the client to authenticate the user.

python

```
def verify_token(token):
    try:
        payload       =       jwt.decode(token,
SECRET_KEY, algorithms=['HS256'])
        return payload['user_id']
    except jwt.ExpiredSignatureError:
        return None  # Token has expired
    except jwt.InvalidTokenError:
        return None  # Invalid token
```

- o **Explanation**:

- jwt.decode() decodes the JWT token and verifies its validity. If the token is valid and not expired, the user_id is returned.

- **Protecting Endpoints with JWT Authentication**: You can protect API endpoints by requiring a valid JWT token to access them. For example:

python

```python
from flask import request

class ProtectedResource(Resource):
    def get(self):
        token = request.headers.get('Authorization')    # Get token from headers
        if not token:
            return {'message': 'Token missing'}, 403

        user_id = verify_token(token)
        if not user_id:
            return {'message': 'Invalid or expired token'}, 403

        return {'message': 'Access granted', 'user_id': user_id}
```

232

```
api.add_resource(ProtectedResource,
'/protected')
```

- o **Explanation**:
    - The `Authorization` header is checked for the JWT token.
    - If the token is missing or invalid, the request is denied (HTTP 403).
    - If the token is valid, access is granted to the resource.

---

4. Project: Build a Task Management API

In this project, you will build a simple task management API using Flask. The API will allow users to:

- Create a task
- View all tasks
- Update a task
- Delete a task
- Authenticate with JWT tokens
- **Step 1: Define the Task Model**: Define a simple in-memory task storage (e.g., a list or dictionary) for storing tasks.

```python
```

```
tasks = {}
task_counter = 1
```

- **Step 2: Define the Task Resource**: Create resources for managing tasks (create, read, update, delete).

```python
class TaskList(Resource):
    def get(self):
        return tasks

    def post(self):
        global task_counter
        data = request.get_json()
        task_name = data.get('task_name')
        tasks[task_counter] =
{'task_name':    task_name,    'status':
'pending'}
        task_counter += 1
        return {'message': 'Task created
successfully'}, 201

class Task(Resource):
    def get(self, task_id):
        task = tasks.get(task_id)
        if task:
            return task
        return {'message': 'Task not
found'}, 404
```

```
    def put(self, task_id):
        data = request.get_json()
        task_name = data.get('task_name')
        if task_id in tasks:
            tasks[task_id]['task_name'] = task_name
            return {'message': 'Task updated successfully'}
            return {'message': 'Task not found'}, 404


    def delete(self, task_id):
        if task_id in tasks:
            del tasks[task_id]
            return {'message': 'Task deleted successfully'}
            return {'message': 'Task not found'}, 404
```

- **Step 3: Add Authentication**: Use JWT to protect task management endpoints, ensuring that only authenticated users can access them.

```python
python


class Login(Resource):
    def post(self):
        data = request.get_json()
```

```
        username = data.get('username')
        if username == 'admin':  # For
simplicity, use a hardcoded user
            token                =
generate_token(user_id=1)
            return {'token': token}
        return  {'message':  'Invalid
credentials'}, 401
```

- **Step 4: Create the Flask App and Add Routes**:

python

```python
app = Flask(__name__)
api = Api(app)

api.add_resource(TaskList, '/tasks')
api.add_resource(Task,
'/task/<int:task_id>')
api.add_resource(Login, '/login')

if __name__ == '__main__':
    app.run(debug=True)
```

Conclusion:

In this chapter, you learned how to build RESTful APIs using Flask. You explored how to handle HTTP methods such as GET, POST, PUT, and DELETE, and how to authenticate users using

JWT tokens. By building a task management API, you gained practical experience in creating API endpoints, managing resources, and securing endpoints with authentication. Flask makes it easy to build RESTful APIs, and with these techniques, you can start building more complex applications with user authentication and data management.

CHAPTER 21

INTRODUCTION TO DJANGO FRAMEWORK

Overview:

Django is a high-level Python web framework that simplifies web development by providing powerful tools and libraries to build scalable and maintainable web applications. It follows the "batteries-included" philosophy, offering built-in solutions for common web development tasks such as database management, user authentication, and URL routing. In this chapter, we will introduce the core concepts of Django and guide you through setting up a Django project, creating models, views, and templates, and building a simple blog application.

Topics Covered:

1. Setting Up Django Projects and Apps

Django projects are containers for your entire web application, while apps are individual components within the project. An app can be a feature like a blog, an authentication system, or a forum.

- **Installing Django**: To install Django, run the following command:

bash

```
pip install django
```

- **Creating a Django Project**: After installing Django, you can create a new project using the `django-admin` tool.

bash

```
django-admin startproject myproject
```

This will create a directory structure for your project:

markdown

```
myproject/
    manage.py
    myproject/
        __init__.py
        settings.py
        urls.py
        wsgi.py
```

- **Creating a Django App**: In Django, an app is a Python package that contains models, views, templates, and static files. To create an app within your project, run:

```bash
```

```
python manage.py startapp blog
```

This will create the following directory structure:

```cpp
```

```
blog/
    __init__.py
    admin.py
    apps.py
    models.py
    views.py
    migrations/
    tests.py
    urls.py
    templates/
    static/
```

- o **Explanation**:
    - `manage.py`: A command-line utility for managing the Django project.
    - `settings.py`: The configuration file for your project.
    - `urls.py`: The URL routing configuration file for your project.
    - `models.py`: Where you define the database models (tables) for your app.

240

- `views.py`: Where you define the logic for handling requests and returning responses.
- `templates/`: A directory where HTML templates are stored.
- `static/`: A directory for static files (e.g., images, JavaScript, CSS).

- **Configuring the App**: Once you've created an app, you need to add it to the `INSTALLED_APPS` list in the `settings.py` file:

```python
INSTALLED_APPS = [
    # Other apps...
    'blog',
]
```

---

2. Working with Models and Views

In Django, models define the structure of your database tables, and views handle user requests and return appropriate responses.

- **Creating Models**: Models are Python classes that define the structure of your database. In the `models.py` file of the `blog` app, define a `Post` model for your blog application:

```python
python

from django.db import models

class Post(models.Model):
    title                                    =
models.CharField(max_length=100)
    content = models.TextField()
    published_at                             =
models.DateTimeField(auto_now_add=True)

    def __str__(self):
        return self.title
```

- o **Explanation**:
  - CharField defines a string field with a maximum length of 100 characters.
  - TextField defines a field for longer text (e.g., the content of the blog post).
  - DateTimeField is used for storing date and time information.

- **Creating Views**: Views in Django are functions or classes that handle HTTP requests and return HTTP responses. A basic view that displays a list of blog posts can be created in views.py:

```python
python
```

```python
from django.shortcuts import render
from .models import Post

def post_list(request):
    posts = Post.objects.all()  # Get all
posts from the database
    return             render(request,
'blog/post_list.html', {'posts': posts})
```

- o **Explanation**:
  - ▪ `Post.objects.all()` retrieves all the posts from the database.
  - ▪ `render()` is a shortcut function that combines a template with context data (in this case, the list of posts) and returns an HTTP response.
- **Configuring URLs**: In Django, you need to define URL patterns to map URLs to views. In the `urls.py` file of your `blog` app, add the following:

```python
python

from django.urls import path
from . import views

urlpatterns = [
    path('',                 views.post_list,
name='post_list'),
]
```

243

o **Explanation**:

- `path('', views.post_list)` maps the root URL (/) to the `post_list` view.

---

3. Using Django Templates and Static Files

Django provides a powerful templating engine that allows you to separate the logic from the presentation of your application. Templates are HTML files that define how the content will be displayed to the user.

- **Creating Templates**: In the `templates` directory of your `blog` app, create a file called `post_list.html` to display the list of blog posts:

html

```html
<!DOCTYPE html>
<html>
<head>
    <title>Blog Posts</title>
</head>
<body>
    <h1>Blog Posts</h1>
    <ul>
        {% for post in posts %}
```

244

```
            <li>
                <strong>{{        post.title
}}</strong><br>
                {{
post.content|truncatewords:20 }}<br>
                <small>{{
post.published_at }}</small>
                </li>
            {% endfor %}
        </ul>
    </body>
    </html>
```

- o **Explanation**:
  - `{% for post in posts %}`: This is a loop that iterates through all the posts passed from the view.
  - `{{ post.title }}`: This displays the title of each post.
  - `{{ post.content|truncatewords:20 }}`: This truncates the content to the first 20 words.
  - `{% endfor %}`: Ends the loop.
- **Using Static Files**: Static files (such as CSS, JavaScript, and images) are stored in the `static` directory. To link a CSS file to your template, you need to load the static files in your template:

245

```
html
```

```
{% load static %}
```

```
<link rel="stylesheet" href="{% static
'css/styles.css' %}">
```

- o **Explanation**:
  - `{% load static %}` loads the static files template tag.
  - `{% static 'css/styles.css' %}` generates the correct URL for the static file.

---

4. Project: Build a Blog Application

In this project, we will build a simple blog application with features such as creating, viewing, and listing blog posts.

- **Step 1: Define the Model**: In `models.py`, define the `Post` model as shown earlier:

```python
class Post(models.Model):
    title                              =
models.CharField(max_length=100)
    content = models.TextField()
```

```
published_at                    =
models.DateTimeField(auto_now_add=True)

    def __str__(self):
        return self.title
```

- **Step 2: Create the View**: In views.py, create a view to list all blog posts:

python

```
def post_list(request):
    posts = Post.objects.all()   # Get all
posts
    return                 render(request,
'blog/post_list.html', {'posts': posts})
```

- **Step 3: Set Up the URL Configuration**: In urls.py, define the URL pattern for the post_list view:

python

```
urlpatterns = [
    path('',                views.post_list,
name='post_list'),
]
```

247

- **Step 4: Create the Template**: In templates/blog/post_list.html, create the HTML structure for displaying the blog posts:

html

```
<!DOCTYPE html>
<html>
<head>
    <title>Blog Posts</title>
</head>
<body>
    <h1>Blog Posts</h1>
    <ul>
        {% for post in posts %}
            <li>
                <strong>{{        post.title
}}</strong><br>
                {{
post.content|truncatewords:20 }}<br>
                <small>{{
post.published_at }}</small>
            </li>
        {% endfor %}
    </ul>
</body>
</html>
```

- **Step 5: Running the Application**: To run the application, execute the following:

```bash

python manage.py runserver
```

Visit `http://127.0.0.1:8000/` in your browser to see the blog posts.

Conclusion:

In this chapter, you learned the fundamentals of web development with **Django**, including how to set up a Django project and app, create models and views, use Django templates to render HTML, and work with static files. You also built a blog application that allows users to view blog posts. Django's powerful features make it a great framework for building robust, scalable web applications quickly and efficiently. With this foundation, you can now explore more advanced topics in Django, such as user authentication, form handling, and deployment.

CHAPTER 22

INTRODUCTION TO WEBSOCKETS WITH PYTHON

Overview:

WebSockets enable real-time, bidirectional communication between a client and server, which is a crucial feature for building dynamic web applications that require constant updates, such as chat apps, live notifications, or collaborative tools. In this chapter, you will learn how to set up WebSocket communication in Python, integrate real-time updates into your web applications, and use **Socket.IO** to make your applications interactive. By the end of the chapter, you will build a real-time chat application that uses WebSockets for live communication between users.

Topics Covered:

1. Setting Up WebSocket Communication in Python

WebSockets are a communication protocol that enables full-duplex communication channels over a single TCP connection. Python has several libraries to help you work with WebSockets, but the most commonly used ones are **websockets** and **socket.io**.

- **Installing the WebSockets Library**: To get started, you need to install the websockets library.

bash

```
pip install websockets
```

- **Creating a Simple WebSocket Server**: The websockets library allows you to create a WebSocket server that can handle multiple connections.

python

```
import asyncio
import websockets

async def echo(websocket, path):
    async for message in websocket:
        await        websocket.send(f"Echo:
{message}")

start_server   =   websockets.serve(echo,
"localhost", 8765)

asyncio.get_event_loop().run_until_comple
te(start_server)
asyncio.get_event_loop().run_forever()
```

o **Explanation**:

- websockets.serve() creates a WebSocket server that listens on localhost:8765.
- The echo function is called whenever a client sends a message to the server. The server then sends the same message back.

- **WebSocket Client**: To connect to the server, create a client that communicates with it.

python

```
import asyncio
import websockets

async def hello():
    uri = "ws://localhost:8765"
    async with websockets.connect(uri) as
websocket:
        await         websocket.send("Hello,
Server!")
        response = await websocket.recv()
        print(response)

asyncio.get_event_loop().run_until_comple
te(hello())
```

- o **Explanation**:

- The client connects to the WebSocket server and sends a message. It then waits for the server to respond.

---

2. Real-Time Updates in Web Apps

WebSockets allow real-time communication, meaning that the server can push data to the client without the client having to request it. This is especially useful in applications like real-time chat, live notifications, or collaborative editing tools.

- **Use Case for Real-Time Updates**: A common use case for WebSockets is a **real-time chat application** where messages are instantly delivered to the users as soon as they are sent, without the need to refresh the page.
- **Push Notifications**: WebSockets can be used to push notifications from the server to the client whenever there is an update. For instance, in a messaging application, the server can notify the client when a new message arrives.

```python
import websockets
import asyncio

async def notify_clients():
```

253

```
    # Here we can simulate new messages
arriving on the server
    while True:
        await asyncio.sleep(5)  # Wait for
5 seconds
        print("New message arrived!")
        # Push a message to all connected
clients
        await websocket.send("New message
notification")

# Connect the clients and push
notifications
asyncio.get_event_loop().run_until_comple
te(notify_clients())
```

3. Using Socket.IO in Python for Real-Time Apps

While `websockets` is great for low-level communication, **Socket.IO** is a higher-level protocol built on top of WebSockets that provides additional features such as automatic reconnections, message broadcasting, and easier event handling. Python has a `python-socketio` library that integrates well with Flask, Django, or any other web framework.

- **Installing Python-SocketIO**: To use Socket.IO, install the `python-socketio` library:

254

```bash
bash

pip install python-socketio
```

- **Setting Up a Socket.IO Server**: You can use **Flask-SocketIO** to create a real-time server with Flask.

```bash
bash

pip install flask flask-socketio
```

- o Example of setting up a Socket.IO server with Flask:

```python
python

from flask import Flask, render_template
from flask_socketio import SocketIO, send

app = Flask(__name__)
socketio = SocketIO(app)

@app.route('/')
def index():
    return render_template('index.html')

@socketio.on('message')
def handle_message(msg):
    print(f"Received message: {msg}")
    send(f"Echo: {msg}")
```

```
if __name__ == '__main__':
    socketio.run(app,    host='localhost',
port=5000)
```

- o **Explanation**:
  - ▪ `Flask-SocketIO` integrates Socket.IO into a Flask app.
  - ▪ The `handle_message` function listens for messages from the client and sends back an echo response.
- **Socket.IO Client**: To interact with the server, you will need a Socket.IO client. This can be done using JavaScript for web clients, but for Python clients, use the `python-socketio` library.

```bash
pip install python-socketio
```

- o Example client:

```python
import socketio

# Connect to the Socket.IO server
sio = socketio.Client()
```

```python
@sio.event
def connect():
    print('Connected to server')


@sio.event
def message(data):
    print(f"Received: {data}")


@sio.event
def disconnect():
    print('Disconnected from server')


sio.connect('http://localhost:5000')
sio.send('Hello, server!')


sio.wait()
```

o **Explanation**:

- The Python Socket.IO client connects to the server, sends a message, and listens for responses.

---

4. Project: Build a Real-Time Chat Application

In this project, we will build a real-time chat application where users can send messages to each other in real-time.

257

- **Step 1: Create the Flask App with Socket.IO Server**: Set up the Flask server and the Socket.IO event handlers for handling incoming and outgoing messages.

python

```python
from flask import Flask, render_template
from flask_socketio import SocketIO, send

app = Flask(__name__)
socketio = SocketIO(app)

@app.route('/')
def index():
    return render_template('index.html')

@socketio.on('message')
def handle_message(msg):
    send(msg, broadcast=True)  # Broadcast
the message to all connected clients

if __name__ == '__main__':
    socketio.run(app)
```

- o **Explanation**:
  - The Flask route / serves the index.html file (which we will create next).

- The `handle_message` function listens for messages from the client and broadcasts them to all connected clients.

- **Step 2: Create the Front-End (index.html)**: Create a simple HTML page where users can send and receive messages.

```
html
```

```html
<!DOCTYPE html>
<html lang="en">
<head>
    <meta charset="UTF-8">
    <meta                   name="viewport"
content="width=device-width,        initial-
scale=1.0">
    <title>Real-Time Chat</title>
    <script
src="https://cdn.socket.io/4.0.1/socket.i
o.min.js"></script>
</head>
<body>
    <h1>Real-Time Chat</h1>
    <ul id="messages"></ul>
    <input  id="messageInput"  type="text"
placeholder="Type a message">
    <button
onclick="sendMessage()">Send</button>
```

```
<script>
    var          socket          =
io.connect('http://localhost:5000');

    socket.on('message', function(msg)
{
        var          li          =
document.createElement('li');
        li.textContent = msg;

document.getElementById('messages').appen
dChild(li);
    });

    function sendMessage() {
        var      message      =
document.getElementById('messageInput').v
alue;
        socket.send(message);  // Send
the message to the server

document.getElementById('messageInput').v
alue = '';  // Clear input field
    }
</script>
</body>
</html>
```

o **Explanation**:

- The client connects to the Flask server using Socket.IO.
- When the user sends a message, it is sent to the server and then broadcast to all connected clients.
- The messages are displayed in an unordered list (`<ul>`).

- **Step 3: Run the Application**: To run the app, execute:

```bash
```

```
python app.py
```

Open `http://localhost:5000/` in multiple browser tabs or different browsers to simulate multiple users chatting in real-time.

Conclusion:

In this chapter, you learned how to use **WebSockets** and **Socket.IO** to build real-time web applications with Python. You explored how to set up WebSocket communication, use Socket.IO for real-time interactions, and build a simple chat application. WebSockets enable powerful features like live updates, notifications, and collaborative tools, making them essential for modern web development. With the knowledge gained in this chapter, you can now build more complex real-time applications

261

such as collaborative editors, live dashboards, and multiplayer games.

CHAPTER 23

CLOUD COMPUTING WITH PYTHON

Overview:

Cloud computing has become a foundational aspect of modern web applications, enabling developers to deploy and manage applications without worrying about the underlying infrastructure. Python is a powerful tool for interacting with cloud platforms and automating cloud-based tasks. In this chapter, we will explore how to use Python for building cloud-based applications. We will cover the basics of cloud platforms such as AWS, Azure, and Google Cloud, automate cloud services using Python, and interact with cloud storage and databases. By the end of this chapter, you will build an application that interacts with cloud APIs, demonstrating how Python can be leveraged for cloud-based solutions.

Topics Covered:

1. Introduction to Cloud Platforms (AWS, Azure, GCP)

Cloud platforms such as **Amazon Web Services (AWS)**, **Microsoft Azure**, and **Google Cloud Platform (GCP)** provide a range of services to help developers build, deploy, and scale applications. These platforms offer compute resources, storage, machine learning, and many other services, which can be integrated into your Python applications.

- **Amazon Web Services (AWS)**: AWS is a comprehensive cloud platform provided by Amazon. It offers a wide array of services such as EC2 (for computing), S3 (for storage), RDS (for databases), and Lambda (for serverless computing).

    - **AWS SDK for Python (Boto3)**: To interact with AWS services, we use `boto3`, the AWS SDK for Python.

      bash

      ```
      pip install boto3
      ```

- **Microsoft Azure**: Azure is Microsoft's cloud platform that provides services like virtual machines (VMs), databases (Azure SQL), and app services. Azure integrates well with Python using the Azure SDK for Python.

- o **Azure SDK for Python**: You can install the Azure SDK for Python using pip:

```bash
pip install azure
```

- **Google Cloud Platform (GCP)**: GCP is Google's cloud offering, which includes services like Compute Engine (VMs), Cloud Storage, and BigQuery. The `google-cloud` library allows Python developers to interact with GCP services.

  - o **Google Cloud SDK for Python**: Install the GCP SDK using pip:

```bash
pip install google-cloud
```

2. Automating Cloud Services with Python

Cloud providers offer APIs that allow you to automate tasks such as provisioning resources, managing storage, or deploying applications. Python can be used to interact with these APIs, making it easier to automate cloud workflows.

- **Automating AWS Services with Boto3**: For example, with `boto3`, you can automate the creation of an S3 bucket (AWS's cloud storage service):

```python
import boto3

# Create an S3 client
s3 = boto3.client('s3')

# Create a new S3 bucket
s3.create_bucket(Bucket='my-new-bucket')

# List all S3 buckets
response = s3.list_buckets()
print(response['Buckets'])
```

  - **Explanation**:
    - `boto3.client('s3')`: Creates an S3 client to interact with AWS S3.
    - `create_bucket()`: Creates a new bucket in S3.
    - `list_buckets()`: Lists all the S3 buckets in your AWS account.
- **Automating Azure Services**: You can interact with Azure services using the Azure SDK. For instance, creating an Azure Blob Storage container:

266

```python
python

from      azure.storage.blob      import
BlobServiceClient

# Connect to Azure Blob Storage
connection_string                      =
"your_connection_string"
blob_service_client                    =
BlobServiceClient.from_connection_string(
connection_string)

# Create a new container
container_name = "mycontainer"
container_client                       =
blob_service_client.create_container(cont
ainer_name)
```

- o **Explanation**:
  - `BlobServiceClient.from_connec` `tion_string(connection_string` `)`: Creates a connection to Azure Blob Storage.
  - `create_container()`: Creates a new container in Azure Blob Storage.
- **Automating GCP Services**: Similarly, you can automate tasks in GCP using the `google-cloud` SDK. For example, creating a new Cloud Storage bucket:

267

```python
from google.cloud import storage

# Initialize a Cloud Storage client
storage_client = storage.Client()

# Create a new bucket
bucket_name = 'my-new-bucket'
bucket = storage_client.create_bucket(bucket_name)
```

- o **Explanation**:
  - `storage.Client()`: Creates a client to interact with GCP Cloud Storage.
  - `create_bucket()`: Creates a new Cloud Storage bucket.

---

3. Working with Cloud Storage and Databases

Python can be used to interact with cloud storage services (e.g., AWS S3, Azure Blob Storage, GCP Cloud Storage) as well as cloud-based databases (e.g., AWS RDS, Azure SQL Database, Google Cloud SQL).

- **Uploading and Downloading Files to/from AWS S3:**

```python
```

```python
import boto3

# Connect to S3
s3 = boto3.client('s3')

# Upload a file to S3
s3.upload_file('local_file.txt', 'my-new-bucket', 'uploaded_file.txt')

# Download a file from S3
s3.download_file('my-new-bucket',
'uploaded_file.txt',
'downloaded_file.txt')
```

- o **Explanation**:
  - `upload_file()`: Uploads a file to the specified S3 bucket.
  - `download_file()`: Downloads a file from the specified S3 bucket.

- **Interacting with AWS RDS (Relational Database Service)**: You can connect to a cloud-based database like Amazon RDS using Python's `psycopg2` library for PostgreSQL or `pymysql` for MySQL.

```bash
pip install psycopg2
python
```

269

```python
import psycopg2

# Connect to AWS RDS PostgreSQL
conn = psycopg2.connect(
    host="your-rds-
instance.amazonaws.com",
    database="your-db-name",
    user="your-username",
    password="your-password"
)

# Create a cursor
cursor = conn.cursor()

# Execute a query
cursor.execute("SELECT        *         FROM
your_table;")
rows = cursor.fetchall()
print(rows)
```

- o **Explanation**:
    - psycopg2.connect(): Connects to the PostgreSQL database on AWS RDS.
    - cursor.execute(): Executes SQL queries on the database.

4. Project: Build an App that Interacts with Cloud APIs

In this project, we will build a Python app that interacts with a cloud service (AWS S3 in this case). The app will allow users to upload, list, and delete files in an S3 bucket.

- **Step 1: Set Up AWS S3**: First, make sure you have an AWS account, and create an S3 bucket where files will be stored. You will need to configure your AWS credentials (AWS_ACCESS_KEY_ID and AWS_SECRET_ACCESS_KEY).

- **Step 2: Create a Python App to Interact with S3**:

```python
python

import boto3
from flask import Flask, request

app = Flask(__name__)

s3 = boto3.client('s3')
BUCKET_NAME = 'my-new-bucket'

@app.route('/upload', methods=['POST'])
def upload_file():
    file = request.files['file']
    file_name = file.filename
    s3.upload_fileobj(file,    BUCKET_NAME,
file_name)
```

271

```
        return  f"File  {file_name}  uploaded
successfully!", 200


@app.route('/list', methods=['GET'])
def list_files():
    response                          =
s3.list_objects_v2(Bucket=BUCKET_NAME)
    file_names = [obj['Key']  for  obj  in
response.get('Contents', [])]
    return {"files": file_names}, 200


@app.route('/delete', methods=['DELETE'])
def delete_file():
    file_name                          =
request.args.get('filename')
    s3.delete_object(Bucket=BUCKET_NAME,
Key=file_name)
    return  f"File  {file_name}  deleted
successfully!", 200


if __name__ == '__main__':
    app.run(debug=True)
```

- o **Explanation**:
  - The app provides three routes: /upload
    for uploading files, /list for listing all
    files in the S3 bucket, and /delete for
    deleting a file from the bucket.

272

- request.files['file'] gets the uploaded file from the request.

- **Step 3: Running the App**: To run the app, execute:

```bash
```

```
python app.py
```

You can interact with the app by sending HTTP requests to http://127.0.0.1:5000/.

Conclusion:

In this chapter, you learned how to use Python for cloud-based applications by interacting with cloud platforms like AWS, Azure, and Google Cloud. You explored automating cloud services using Python, working with cloud storage and databases, and leveraging cloud APIs. Finally, you applied these skills by building an app that interacts with cloud APIs to upload, list, and delete files in AWS S3. Cloud computing allows you to scale applications efficiently and is a critical skill for modern developers. With the tools and techniques learned in this chapter, you can start building powerful cloud-based applications with Python.

CHAPTER 24

WEB DEVELOPMENT BEST PRACTICES

Overview:

Building a web application is not just about getting it to work, but also about ensuring that the code is clean, maintainable, and scalable. Writing web applications with best practices helps improve collaboration, ease of maintenance, and future scalability. In this chapter, we will explore key best practices in web development, such as organizing your code effectively, using version control with Git, writing secure applications, and ensuring your app can scale as needed. By the end of this chapter, you will apply these practices by refactoring an existing Python web application.

Topics Covered:

1. Code Structure and Organization

A well-organized codebase is crucial for long-term maintainability and ease of collaboration. Properly structuring

274

your web app's files and directories helps developers navigate and manage the code more effectively.

- **Directory Structure**: For a clean and maintainable codebase, you should separate different components of your web application (e.g., models, views, templates, static files, etc.) into dedicated directories. Here is a typical structure for a Flask web app:

```php
myapp/
├── app/
│   ├── __init__.py          # Initializes the app
│   ├── routes.py            # Handles routing (views)
│   ├── models.py            # Database models
│   ├── templates/           # HTML templates
│   └── static/              # Static files (CSS, JS, images)
├── config.py                # Configuration file (DB, API keys)
├── requirements.txt         # Project dependencies
└── run.py                   # Entry point to run the app
```

- o **Explanation**:

- ▪ `__init__.py`: Initializes the Flask app and sets up configurations.
- ▪ `routes.py`: Contains route definitions and view functions.
- ▪ `models.py`: Defines the database models and schema.
- ▪ `templates/`: Stores HTML templates used by Flask to render content.
- ▪ `static/`: Contains static files like CSS, JavaScript, and images.
- ▪ `config.py`: Stores configuration details such as database URI or secret keys.
- ▪ `requirements.txt`: Lists all the external dependencies required for the app.
- **Modularity**: Keeping code modular by splitting functionality into smaller, reusable components is essential for scalability and maintainability. For example:
  - o Create separate modules for database handling (`models.py`), business logic (`services.py`), and views (`routes.py`).
  - o Each module should have a clear responsibility, making it easier to extend and refactor.

2. Version Control with Git

Version control is crucial for tracking changes in your code, collaborating with other developers, and maintaining a history of changes. Git is the most widely used version control system in software development.

- **Setting Up Git**: Initialize a Git repository in your project directory:

```bash
git init
```

- **Basic Git Commands**:
  - **git add**: Stages changes for commit:

  ```bash
  git add .
  ```

  - **git commit**: Commits the staged changes to the repository:

  ```bash
  git commit -m "Initial commit"
  ```

○ **git status**: Checks the status of your files (modified, staged, untracked):

```bash
git status
```

○ **git log**: Shows the commit history:

```bash
git log
```

○ **git push**: Pushes local commits to a remote repository:

```bash
git push origin master
```

- **Using Branches**: Working with branches helps you develop new features or fix bugs without affecting the main codebase. It is a good practice to create a new branch for each new feature or bug fix:

```bash
git checkout -b feature/new-feature
```

After working on the feature, commit and merge it back to the main branch:

```bash
git checkout master
git merge feature/new-feature
```

- **Using GitHub or GitLab**: Hosting your repository on platforms like GitHub or GitLab allows for collaboration, code reviews, and version tracking across teams.

---

3. Writing Secure and Scalable Applications

Security and scalability are two critical aspects of web development. Here are some best practices to ensure that your web applications are secure and scalable.

- **Security Best Practices**:
  - **Input Validation and Sanitization**: Always validate and sanitize user inputs to prevent attacks like **SQL injection** and **Cross-Site Scripting (XSS)**.
  - **Password Hashing**: Never store plain-text passwords. Use libraries like **bcrypt** or **argon2** to hash passwords before storing them in the database.

279

- o **CSRF Protection**: Cross-Site Request Forgery (CSRF) attacks can be mitigated using CSRF tokens for form submissions in web applications.
- o **HTTPS**: Always use HTTPS to secure communications between the client and server. SSL certificates encrypt data, protecting sensitive information from being intercepted.
- o **Access Control**: Implement role-based access control (RBAC) to restrict access to sensitive parts of the application based on user roles (e.g., admin, user).
- o **Example** (Password Hashing with bcrypt in Python):

```python
from bcrypt import hashpw, gensalt, checkpw

password = 'securepassword'
hashed_password                        =
hashpw(password.encode('utf-8'),
gensalt())

# To verify the password
checkpw(password.encode('utf-8'),
hashed_password)
```

- **Scalability Best Practices**:
  - o **Load Balancing**: Distribute traffic across multiple servers to ensure that no single server is overwhelmed.
  - o **Database Optimization**: Use indexing, caching, and query optimization to improve database performance.
  - o **Caching**: Cache frequently accessed data using tools like **Redis** or **Memcached** to reduce load on the database.
  - o **Asynchronous Processing**: Use task queues (e.g., **Celery**) to handle long-running tasks asynchronously without blocking the main application.

4. Project: Refactor an Existing Python Web Application

In this project, you will refactor an existing Python web application to apply the best practices we've discussed. This includes improving the code structure, adding version control, enhancing security, and ensuring scalability.

- **Step 1: Refactor Code Structure**: Review the codebase and organize it into separate modules (e.g., models, routes, services). Ensure each module has a clear responsibility.

For example, move the business logic (e.g., processing user data) into a `services.py` file, and keep the route definitions in the `routes.py` file.

- **Step 2: Add Version Control with Git**: Initialize a Git repository and commit the changes. Use meaningful commit messages to track progress.

bash

```
git init
git add .
git commit -m "Refactor code structure and
add version control"
```

- **Step 3: Implement Security Features**:
  - o Add input validation and sanitization to protect against SQL injection and XSS.
  - o Implement password hashing (e.g., using bcrypt).
  - o Use HTTPS and implement CSRF protection for form submissions.
- **Step 4: Improve Scalability**:
  - o Introduce caching to store frequently accessed data.
  - o Optimize database queries and add indexes to improve query performance.
  - o Set up a task queue (e.g., **Celery**) for asynchronous tasks.

- **Step 5: Document the Code**: Add docstrings to functions and classes to improve code readability and maintainability. You can use tools like **Sphinx** to generate documentation from docstrings.

Conclusion:

In this chapter, we explored the best practices for writing clean, maintainable, and scalable web applications. We covered code structure and organization, the importance of version control with Git, and how to write secure applications. Additionally, we applied these best practices by refactoring an existing Python web application. By following these practices, you ensure that your web applications are not only functional but also secure, scalable, and easy to maintain over time. Implementing these principles early in the development process will save time and resources as your application grows.

CHAPTER 25

PYTHON FOR IOT (INTERNET OF THINGS) PROJECTS

Overview:

The Internet of Things (IoT) refers to the interconnection of everyday devices (such as sensors, lights, and appliances) to the internet, enabling them to collect and exchange data. Python is one of the most popular programming languages for IoT due to its simplicity, flexibility, and vast library ecosystem. In this chapter, we will explore how Python can be used to interact with IoT devices. You will learn how to set up IoT devices, communicate with them using protocols such as MQTT and HTTP, and collect and control data from sensors. Finally, we will build a project that involves creating an IoT-based weather monitoring system.

Topics Covered:

1. Setting Up IoT Devices with Python

Setting up IoT devices involves configuring sensors, microcontrollers, and communication modules to interact with the

Python code running on a Raspberry Pi, Arduino, or other microcontrollers.

- **IoT Devices**:
    - **Raspberry Pi**: A popular microcomputer that supports Python and can be used to interact with sensors and actuators.
    - **Arduino**: A microcontroller often used for sensor data acquisition and device control. It can communicate with Python via serial communication.
    - **ESP8266/ESP32**: Low-cost microcontrollers with built-in Wi-Fi, commonly used for IoT projects.
- **Setting Up a Raspberry Pi**: To use a Raspberry Pi for IoT projects, you need to install the necessary software, including Python and libraries like **RPi.GPIO** for controlling GPIO pins.
    - **Installing Python**: Raspberry Pi comes with Python pre-installed, but you can ensure you have the latest version with:

```bash
sudo apt update
sudo apt install python3
```

- o **Setting Up GPIO Pins**: Use the **RPi.GPIO** library to control Raspberry Pi's GPIO pins:

```bash
pip install RPi.GPIO
```

Example of controlling an LED with Raspberry Pi:

```python
import RPi.GPIO as GPIO
import time

GPIO.setmode(GPIO.BCM)
GPIO.setup(18, GPIO.OUT)

# Turn the LED on
GPIO.output(18, GPIO.HIGH)
time.sleep(1)

# Turn the LED off
GPIO.output(18, GPIO.LOW)
GPIO.cleanup()
```

2. Communication Protocols (MQTT, HTTP)

Communication between IoT devices is facilitated by various protocols. The two most common protocols are **MQTT** (Message Queuing Telemetry Transport) and **HTTP** (Hypertext Transfer Protocol).

- **MQTT**: MQTT is a lightweight, publish-subscribe messaging protocol used for low-bandwidth, high-latency networks, making it ideal for IoT devices.
  - **Installing Paho-MQTT**: The **Paho MQTT** library is used to communicate with MQTT brokers. Install it using pip:

    ```bash
    pip install paho-mqtt
    ```

  - **Basic MQTT Client**: Here's an example of a simple MQTT client in Python that connects to a broker and sends data.

    ```python
    import paho.mqtt.client as mqtt

    broker = "mqtt.eclipse.org"
    topic = "iot/temperature"
    ```

```python
# Callback when the client connects
to the broker
def on_connect(client, userdata,
flags, rc):
    print(f"Connected with result
code {rc}")
    client.publish(topic, "25.5")  #
Publish temperature data


# Create MQTT client
client = mqtt.Client()
client.on_connect = on_connect
client.connect(broker, 1883, 60)


# Start the MQTT loop
client.loop_forever()
```

- o **Explanation**:
  - `client.connect()` connects to the MQTT broker.
  - `client.publish()` sends the temperature data to the specified topic.
- **HTTP**: HTTP is a request-response protocol commonly used to interact with REST APIs. It's often used for cloud-based IoT applications.
  - o **HTTP Requests with Python**: The **requests** library is commonly used to send HTTP requests.

```bash
```

```
pip install requests
```

o **Sending Data to an HTTP Server**: You can use Python's `requests` module to send sensor data to an HTTP server or cloud service.

```python
python

import requests

url = "https://api.weather.com"
data    =    {'temperature':    25.5,
'humidity': 60}
response    =    requests.post(url,
json=data)

if response.status_code == 200:
    print("Data sent successfully!")
else:
    print(f"Failed   to   send   data.
Status                         code:
{response.status_code}")
```

3. Reading Sensor Data and Controlling Devices

Python can be used to interact with various sensors (e.g., temperature, humidity, motion) and control devices (e.g., motors, lights) in an IoT system.

- **Reading Data from Sensors**: Many sensors communicate over protocols like **I2C**, **SPI**, or **serial**. For example, reading temperature data from a DHT11 sensor:
  - **Installing the DHT Library**:

    ```bash
    pip install Adafruit_DHT
    ```

  - **Reading Temperature and Humidity**:

    ```python
    import Adafruit_DHT

    sensor = Adafruit_DHT.DHT11
    pin = 4  # GPIO pin where the sensor is connected

    humidity, temperature = Adafruit_DHT.read_retry(sensor, pin)
    ```

```python
if humidity is not None and
temperature is not None:
    print(f"Temp:      {temperature}C
Humidity: {humidity}%")
else:
    print("Failed to retrieve data
from sensor")
```

- **Controlling Devices**: To control devices like motors or LEDs, you can use the GPIO pins of the Raspberry Pi or other microcontrollers. For example, controlling a motor using PWM (Pulse Width Modulation):

```python
python

import RPi.GPIO as GPIO
from time import sleep

motor_pin = 17  # GPIO pin where the motor
is connected

GPIO.setmode(GPIO.BCM)
GPIO.setup(motor_pin, GPIO.OUT)
pwm_motor = GPIO.PWM(motor_pin, 100)  # Set
PWM frequency to 100 Hz
pwm_motor.start(0)   # Start PWM with 0%
duty cycle

# Increase motor speed over time
```

```
for speed in range(0, 101, 10):
    pwm_motor.ChangeDutyCycle(speed)
    sleep(1)

pwm_motor.stop()
GPIO.cleanup()
```

---

4. Project: Build an IoT-Based Weather Monitoring System

In this project, we will build an IoT-based weather monitoring system that collects temperature and humidity data from a sensor and sends it to the cloud via an HTTP or MQTT protocol.

- **Step 1: Set Up the Sensor**: Connect a DHT11 or DHT22 sensor to your Raspberry Pi (or other microcontroller) to read temperature and humidity data.
- **Step 2: Install Libraries**: Install the necessary libraries to read data from the sensor and communicate with the cloud.

```bash
pip install Adafruit_DHT paho-mqtt requests
```

- **Step 3: Create a Python Script for Data Collection and Communication**:

```python
python

import Adafruit_DHT
import paho.mqtt.client as mqtt
import requests
import time

# Sensor setup
sensor = Adafruit_DHT.DHT11
pin = 4  # GPIO pin

# MQTT setup
broker = "mqtt.eclipse.org"
topic = "iot/weather"

# Cloud API setup
api_url = "https://api.weather.com"

# MQTT client setup
def on_connect(client, userdata, flags, rc):
    print(f"Connected to {broker} with result code {rc}")

client = mqtt.Client()
client.on_connect = on_connect
client.connect(broker, 1883, 60)
client.loop_start()
```

```python
# Main loop to read sensor data and send it
while True:
    humidity, temperature = Adafruit_DHT.read_retry(sensor, pin)

    if humidity is not None and temperature is not None:
        # Publish data to MQTT broker
        client.publish(topic, f"Temp: {temperature}C, Humidity: {humidity}%")

        # Send data to cloud API via HTTP
        payload = {'temperature': temperature, 'humidity': humidity}
        response = requests.post(api_url, json=payload)

        if response.status_code == 200:
            print("Data sent to cloud successfully")
        else:
            print("Failed to send data to cloud")

    time.sleep(5)  # Wait 5 seconds before reading data again
```

- **Step 4: Run the Application**: Run the Python script to start reading data from the sensor and sending it to the MQTT broker and cloud server.

Conclusion:

In this chapter, we learned how to use Python for IoT (Internet of Things) projects. You explored how to set up IoT devices, communicate with them using protocols like MQTT and HTTP, and read sensor data. We also demonstrated how to build a simple IoT-based weather monitoring system, where data from sensors is collected and sent to the cloud. Python's versatility makes it an excellent choice for IoT development, allowing you to create powerful and scalable IoT applications with ease.

CHAPTER 26

DEPLOYMENT AND SCALING PYTHON APPLICATIONS

Overview:

Deploying and scaling Python applications is a critical skill for moving from development to production. In this chapter, we will explore various tools and techniques for deploying Python web applications to the cloud, using containerization with Docker, and scaling applications using Kubernetes. By the end of this chapter, you will have hands-on experience deploying a Python web app to Heroku, a popular platform-as-a-service (PaaS) that simplifies app deployment.

Topics Covered:

1. Setting Up Cloud Servers (e.g., AWS, Heroku)

Cloud platforms like AWS and Heroku provide resources to host and run web applications. In this section, we'll explore how to deploy a Python web app to **Heroku** and **AWS EC2**.

- **Deploying to Heroku**: Heroku is a cloud platform that simplifies the deployment process, especially for web applications. It abstracts away infrastructure management, allowing developers to focus on their code.

  o **Setting Up Heroku**: First, sign up for a Heroku account at https://www.heroku.com/. Then, install the Heroku CLI to interact with Heroku from the command line:

  ```bash
  ```

  ```bash
  curl                    https://cli-
  assets.heroku.com/install.sh | sh
  ```

  o **Deploying a Python Application to Heroku**:

  1. **Create a `requirements.txt` File**: This file contains the list of dependencies for your Python app.

     ```bash
     ```

     ```bash
     pip freeze > requirements.txt
     ```

  2. **Create a `Procfile`**: The `Procfile` tells Heroku how to run your application. For a Flask app, it should look like this:

     ```makefile
     ```

```
web: python app.py
```

3. **Create a Git Repository**: Initialize a Git repository and commit your changes.

bash

```
git init
git add .
git commit -m "Initial commit"
```

4. **Deploy to Heroku**: Log in to Heroku and create a new app:

bash

```
heroku login
heroku create your-app-name
```

Push your app to Heroku:

bash

```
git push heroku master
```

5. **Open the App**: Once the deployment is complete, open the app in your browser:

bash

```
heroku open
```

- **Deploying to AWS EC2**: AWS provides cloud servers (EC2 instances) where you can deploy your applications. You'll need to configure an EC2 instance and SSH into it to deploy your Python web app.

  o **Step 1: Launch an EC2 Instance**:
    - Sign in to the AWS Management Console and launch a new EC2 instance.
    - Choose an Ubuntu AMI (Amazon Machine Image) for the server.
    - Select an instance type (e.g., `t2.micro` for free-tier usage).
    - Create a new security group to allow HTTP (port 80) and SSH (port 22) access.

  o **Step 2: SSH into the EC2 Instance**: Use the following command to SSH into the instance:

```
bash
```

```
ssh -i "your-key.pem" ubuntu@your-
ec2-ip
```

  o **Step 3: Install Dependencies**:
    - Update the instance and install required packages:

```bash
sudo apt update
sudo apt install python3-pip
python3-dev nginx
```

- **Step 4: Deploy Your Python App**:
  - Upload your Python app to the EC2 instance (using SCP or Git).
  - Set up a WSGI server (e.g., **Gunicorn**) and configure Nginx to proxy HTTP requests to your app.

---

2. Using Docker for Containerization

Docker allows you to package your application and all its dependencies into a container, which ensures that the app will run consistently across different environments. This makes it easier to deploy and scale applications.

- **Installing Docker**: Install Docker by following the instructions on the official Docker website.
- **Creating a Dockerfile**: A `Dockerfile` contains instructions to build a Docker image for your Python web app. Here's an example `Dockerfile` for a Flask app:

```Dockerfile
```

```
# Use an official Python runtime as a
parent image
FROM python:3.8-slim

# Set the working directory in the
container
WORKDIR /app

# the current directory contents into the
container
 . /app

# Install any needed packages specified in
requirements.txt
RUN pip install --no-cache-dir -r
requirements.txt

# Make port 5000 available to the world
outside this container
EXPOSE 5000

# Define environment variable
ENV NAME World

# Run app.py when the container launches
CMD ["python", "app.py"]
```

- **Building and Running the Docker Image**:

1. **Build the Docker Image**:

```bash
bash
```

```bash
docker build -t my-python-app .
```

2. **Run the Docker Container**:

```bash
bash
```

```bash
docker run -p 5000:5000 my-python-app
```

This will run the application inside a Docker container and map port 5000 from the container to port 5000 on your local machine.

- **Docker Compose for Multi-Container Applications**: If your app requires multiple services (e.g., a web server and a database), you can use Docker Compose to manage multiple containers.

Example `docker-compose.yml`:

```yaml
yaml
```

```yaml
version: '3'
services:
  web:
    build: .
```

```
ports:
  - "5000:5000"
db:
  image: postgres
  environment:
    POSTGRES_PASSWORD: example
```

To start the application:

```bash
```

```
docker-compose up
```

---

3. Scaling Applications with Kubernetes

Kubernetes is an open-source platform for automating the deployment, scaling, and management of containerized applications. It allows you to run and manage Docker containers at scale across clusters of machines.

- **Installing Kubernetes**: You can install Kubernetes on your local machine using **Minikube** for development purposes or deploy it on cloud platforms like AWS, GCP, or Azure.

```bash
```

```
brew install minikube   # For macOS
```

303

o **Start a Local Kubernetes Cluster**:

```bash
bash

minikube start
```

- **Creating a Kubernetes Deployment**: A deployment in Kubernetes manages a set of replicas of your application to ensure high availability and scaling.

Example Kubernetes deployment YAML file for a Python web app:

```yaml
yaml

apiVersion: apps/v1
kind: Deployment
metadata:
  name: python-web-app
spec:
  replicas: 3
  selector:
    matchLabels:
      app: python-web-app
  template:
    metadata:
      labels:
        app: python-web-app
    spec:
```

```
containers:
- name: python-web-app
  image: my-python-app:latest
  ports:
  - containerPort: 5000
```

- o **Explanation**:
  - `replicas: 3`: Ensures there are 3 replicas of the app running.
  - `image: my-python-app:latest`: Uses the Docker image built earlier.
  - `containerPort: 5000`: Maps the container's port 5000 to the host machine.

- **Creating a Kubernetes Service**: Expose the application to external traffic using a Kubernetes service:

yaml

```
apiVersion: v1
kind: Service
metadata:
  name: python-web-app-service
spec:
  selector:
    app: python-web-app
  ports:
    - protocol: TCP
      port: 80
```

305

```
      targetPort: 5000
   type: LoadBalancer
```

- o **Explanation**:
  - The service allows external traffic to access the app through port 80 and forwards it to the containers running the app on port 5000.

- **Deploying to Kubernetes**: Once the YAML files are created, you can apply them to the Kubernetes cluster:

bash

```
kubectl apply -f deployment.yaml
kubectl apply -f service.yaml
```

- o **Scaling the Application**: To scale the application (e.g., increase replicas), you can use the following command:

bash

```
kubectl scale deployment python-web-
app --replicas=5
```

4. Project: Deploy a Python Web App to Heroku

In this project, we will deploy a simple Python web app to Heroku, which will allow us to focus on the deployment process without managing server infrastructure.

- **Step 1: Prepare Your Web App**: Ensure that your Python app has a `requirements.txt` file and a `Procfile` (as discussed earlier).
- **Step 2: Initialize a Git Repository**: Initialize a Git repository if you haven't done so already:

bash

```
git init
git add .
git commit -m "Initial commit"
```

- **Step 3: Deploy to Heroku**:
  - o Log in to Heroku and create a new app:

    bash

    ```
    heroku login
    heroku create my-python-web-app
    ```

  - o Push the app to Heroku:

    bash

307

```
git push heroku master
```

o   Once deployed, open the app in a browser:

```
bash
```

```
heroku open
```

Conclusion:

In this chapter, you learned how to deploy and scale Python applications using various tools and platforms. We covered how to deploy a Python web app to **Heroku**, use **Docker** for containerization, and scale applications with **Kubernetes**. These deployment strategies ensure that your applications are scalable, manageable, and ready for production. With this knowledge, you can deploy your Python applications to any cloud platform and scale them as needed.

CHAPTER 27

FINAL PROJECT: BUILD A COMPLETE PYTHON APPLICATION

Overview:

In this final chapter, you will apply all the concepts you've learned throughout the course to build a comprehensive Python application. This capstone project will require you to plan, design, and implement a real-world Python application, focusing on structuring the code, applying Object-Oriented Programming (OOP) principles, testing, deploying, and maintaining the application. By the end of this chapter, you will have developed a complete Python-based application, such as an **e-commerce platform**, demonstrating your understanding of key development practices.

Topics Covered:

1. Planning and Designing a Real-World Python Application

Before diving into the code, planning and designing the application is crucial. This stage helps define the scope, requirements, and functionality of the project. It also sets the foundation for the application's architecture.

- **Defining the Problem and Scope**: Start by identifying the problem your application will solve. For instance, if you're building an **e-commerce platform**, consider the following:
  - Who are the users (customers, admins)?
  - What features are needed (product listing, shopping cart, checkout process, user authentication)?
  - What are the expected outcomes (users should be able to purchase items, admins should manage the inventory)?
- **Designing the Architecture**: Once the requirements are clear, design the architecture of the application. Break it down into key components, such as:
  - **Frontend**: User interface (UI) for customers and admins.
  - **Backend**: Logic to handle user authentication, product management, orders, and payment.

- o **Database**: A database to store user data, product details, orders, etc.
- o **APIs**: APIs for interacting with the frontend and external services (e.g., payment gateways).
- **Database Schema Design**: Design the database schema to represent the entities in the application. For example, in an e-commerce platform, you might need tables like:
  - o **Users**: Stores user details (name, email, password).
  - o **Products**: Stores product details (name, description, price, stock).
  - o **Orders**: Stores information about user orders (product, quantity, total price).
  - o **Shopping Cart**: Temporary storage for items added to the cart before purchase.

2. Structuring the Project and Applying OOP Principles

To maintain readability and ease of future modifications, structure the project logically. Organizing your code effectively and using Object-Oriented Programming (OOP) principles will allow for clean, modular, and reusable code.

- **Organizing the Project Files**: Organize the project into logical modules. A typical structure for an e-commerce platform might look like this:

```php
e-commerce/
├── app/
│   ├── __init__.py
│   ├── models.py          # Contains database models
│   ├── routes.py          # Contains route definitions for the app
│   ├── forms.py           # Contains form handling (e.g., user registration, checkout)
│   ├── views.py           # Contains business logic (e.g., adding products, processing orders)
│   └── templates/         # HTML templates for rendering views
├── static/                # Static files (CSS, JavaScript, images)
├── config.py              # Configuration settings (e.g., database URI, secret keys)
├── requirements.txt       # Project dependencies
└── run.py                 # Entry point to run the app
```

- **Applying OOP Principles**: Use OOP principles such as **encapsulation**, **inheritance**, and **polymorphism** to create reusable, modular components. For example, in the e-commerce app, you could define:

- **User class**: Handles user-related operations (login, registration).
- **Product class**: Manages product data and business logic (e.g., availability, pricing).
- **Order class**: Handles order processing, including calculating the total price and tracking status.
- **Payment class**: Manages payment transactions.

Example of an OOP-based class for `Product`:

python

```python
class Product:
    def __init__(self, product_id, name,
description, price, stock):
        self.product_id = product_id
        self.name = name
        self.description = description
        self.price = price
        self.stock = stock

    def update_stock(self, quantity):
        if self.stock >= quantity:
            self.stock -= quantity
            return True
        else:
            return False
```

313

```
def __str__(self):
    return          f"{self.name}        -
{self.description} (${self.price})"
```

- o **Encapsulation**: The internal data (e.g., `stock`) is hidden from outside access and can only be modified through methods (e.g., `update_stock`).
- o **Inheritance**: You could have subclasses such as `ElectronicProduct` or `ClothingProduct` that inherit from `Product` and add specific behaviors or attributes.
- o **Polymorphism**: Methods like `apply_discount()` could be overridden in subclasses to apply different discount logic for different product types.

---

3. Testing, Deploying, and Maintaining the Application

Testing, deployment, and maintenance are crucial aspects of delivering a production-ready application.

- **Testing the Application**:
  - o **Unit Testing**: Write unit tests for individual components like models, views, and forms. Use

frameworks such as `unittest` or `pytest` to write automated tests.

- o **Integration Testing**: Test how different parts of the application work together. For example, test that the order process works end-to-end, from adding items to the cart to processing the payment.

- o **Mocking External Services**: If your app interacts with external APIs (e.g., payment gateways), use mocking tools like `unittest.mock` to simulate responses from these services during testing.

Example test for the `Product` class:

python

```python
import unittest

class TestProduct(unittest.TestCase):
    def test_update_stock(self):
        product = Product(1, "Laptop",
"High-end gaming laptop", 1500, 10)

self.assertTrue(product.update_stock(5))
        self.assertEqual(product.stock, 5)
```

```
    def
test_update_stock_insufficient(self):
        product   =   Product(2,   "Mouse",
"Wireless mouse", 20, 5)


self.assertFalse(product.update_stock(6))
```

- **Deploying the Application**:
  - o **Deploy to Heroku**: Use **Heroku** for a simple, PaaS-based deployment, which is perfect for small-to-medium-sized applications.
  - o **Dockerizing the Application**: Containerize your app using **Docker** for consistent environments and scalability.
  - o **Deploy to AWS EC2**: Set up an EC2 instance, install dependencies, and configure a web server (e.g., Nginx) to serve your app.

Example Dockerfile for the e-commerce app:

```
Dockerfile


FROM python:3.8-slim


WORKDIR /app
 . /app


RUN   pip   install   --no-cache-dir   -r
requirements.txt
```

```
EXPOSE 5000

CMD ["python", "run.py"]
```

- o **Continuous Deployment (CI/CD)**: Set up a CI/CD pipeline (e.g., using GitHub Actions or CircleCI) to automatically deploy changes to production whenever updates are pushed to your repository.

- **Maintaining the Application**:
  - o **Monitoring**: Use tools like **Sentry** or **Prometheus** to monitor the application for errors and performance issues.
  - o **Log Management**: Ensure your app logs important events and errors, which will be helpful for debugging and optimizing performance.
  - o **Updating and Refactoring**: Continuously improve the codebase by refactoring and adding new features, and ensure backward compatibility with older versions.

---

4. Project: Build a Python-Based E-Commerce Platform

In this project, you will build a full-fledged e-commerce platform. This project will help you apply the concepts covered in this

317

chapter and incorporate everything you have learned throughout the course.

- **Step 1: Define the Features**:
    - ○ **User Authentication**: Allow users to register, log in, and manage their profile.
    - ○ **Product Management**: Allow admins to add, update, and remove products.
    - ○ **Shopping Cart**: Enable users to add products to the cart and proceed to checkout.
    - ○ **Order Management**: Handle order creation, payment processing, and order history.
    - ○ **Payment Integration**: Integrate a payment gateway (e.g., Stripe or PayPal) to handle payments.
- **Step 2: Design the Database Models**: Design the models to represent users, products, orders, and payments. Use a relational database like **PostgreSQL** or **MySQL** to store the data.

Example model for `Product`:

`python`

```
class Product:
    def    __init__(self,    id,    name,
description, price, stock):
        self.id = id
```

```
        self.name = name
        self.description = description
        self.price = price
        self.stock = stock


    def save(self):
        # Logic to save the product to the
database
        pass


    def update(self):
        # Logic to update the product in
the database
        pass
```

- **Step 3: Implement the Views and Routes**: Use Flask or Django to define views for displaying products, adding items to the cart, and processing orders.

- **Step 4: Test the Application**: Write unit tests to ensure that individual components of the application work as expected.

- **Step 5: Deploy the Application**: Deploy the application to a cloud platform like **Heroku**, **AWS**, or **Docker**.

Conclusion:

In this final chapter, you have built a complete Python web application by planning, designing, and implementing an e-commerce platform (or another application of your choice). You applied the concepts of modular design, OOP, testing, deployment, and scaling. By completing this project, you have not only reinforced your knowledge of Python web development but also gained hands-on experience that will serve you well in future real-world projects. With the skills learned in this chapter, you can now confidently build, deploy, and maintain robust and scalable Python web applications.

www.ingramcontent.com/pod-product-compliance
Lightning Source LLC
La Vergne TN
LVHW051431050326
832903LV00030BD/3033